ISBN 978-0-260-63319-4
PIBN 10960872

Historic, archived document

Do not assume content reflects current
scientific knowledge, policies, or practices.

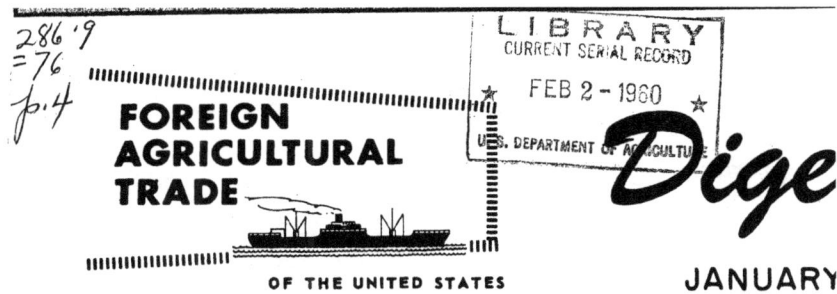

FOREIGN AGRICULTURAL TRADE

Digest

OF THE UNITED STATES

JANUARY

Issued monthly by Foreign Agricultural Service, United States Department of Agi
Washington 25, D.C. Free within U.S. on request. Also available are mon
yearly Foreign Agricultural Trade Statistical Reports, containing detailed s
on quantity and value of exports and imports.

EXPORT HIGHLIGHTS

July-November agricultural exports were 9 percent greater in 1959
the same period of 1958. Exports during July-November were valued
million in 1959 and $1,605 million in 1958. Largest percentage ga
curred in vegetable oils and oilseeds (45 percent), animals and pr
(28 percent), feed grains (13 percent), and fruits and vegetables
cent). After unusually heavy exports in November, cotton shipment
November were behind by only 8 percent. Wheat and tobacco shipmen
each down by 5 percent.

U.S. agricultural exports, July-November

Commodity	1958-59 1/	1959-60	Chg.
	$ Million		%
Cotton	191	175	- 8
Grains & feeds 2/	588	612	+ 4
Wheat & flour 2/	279	265	- 5
Feed grains 2/ 3/	214	241	+13
Rice, milled 2/	48	49	+ 2
Tobacco, unmfd.	203	193	- 5
Veg. oils & seeds 2/	173	251	+45
Soybeans	89	124	+39
Ed. veg. oils 2/ 4/	51	89	+75
Fruits & preps. 2/	108	119	+10
Vegs. & preps. 2/	52	61	+17
Animals & prods. 2/	195	249	+28
Fats & oils	64	77	+20
Meats & products	39	50	+28
Hides & skins	22	29	+32
Dairy products 2/	40	53	+33
Private relief 5/	52	43	-17
Other 2/	43	49	+14
TOTAL	1,605	1,752	+ 9

1/ Partly revised. 2/ Excludes private
relief. 3/ Excludes products. 4/ Cottonseed and soybean. 5/ Mostly CCC donations.

November exports in 195
percent above those of
earlier. Exports total
million in 1959 compare
$342 million in 1958.
cotton, feed grains, ri
table oils and oilseeds
vegetables, and animal
were partly offset by d
in wheat and tobacco.

Government export progr
counted for one-third o
September shipments. F
under Public Law 480 ar
Security programs amour
$330 million in the Jul
ber quarter of fiscal y
$35 million higher than
like quarter of 1959.
est change was the $36
gain in barter which to
million in July-Septemb
Exports of wheat and fl
sented 40 percent of Go
financed exports; feed

grain products, including rice, 22 percent; vegetable oils and oilseeds, 16 percent; cotton, 8 percent; and other commodities (principally tobacco and dairy products) 14 percent.

COTTON   Cotton exports in November exceeded 650 thousand bales. Exports, excluding linters, amounted to 652 thousand running bales in November 1959, more than double the 314 thousand in November 1958. November 1959 exports were 66 percent ahead of October's 392 thousand bales. Some of the factors favoring increased shipments this year over last are (1) more competitive U. S. prices at lower levels, (2) increased foreign consumption, and (3) reduced foreign production and beginning stocks.

GRAINS   Wheat export prospects for this fiscal year have improved. Wheat exports for fiscal year 1960, including USDA welfare donations, now are expected to approach last year's 443 million bushels. The previous forecast, made in November 1959, was 410 million bushels. The upward revision in the export estimate results primarily from new agreements under Title I of Public Law 480, such as that with Turkey, which were not anticipated earlier in the year. July-November 1959 shipments of about 168 million bushels, including donations, were about equal to exports during the same period in the previous year. November shipments, including donations, were 30 million bushels in 1959 compared with 34 million bushels in 1958.

November feed grain exports continued at high level. Exports in November 1959 amounted to 1,191 thousand short tons, excluding USDA welfare donations, compared with 981 thousand in November 1958. July-November shipments totaled 5.6 million tons in 1959 compared with 4.7 million in 1958. The improvement in exports represents mainly continuing increased needs due to expanding livestock and poultry production abroad; however, the drought in Europe also has helped to raise exports.

Increase in milled rice exports is accounted for by Asia, Europe, and Africa. July-November 1959 exports, excluding USDA welfare donations, totaled 745 million pounds, 20 percent greater than the 620 million pounds a year earlier.

TOBACCO   July-November tobacco export volume ran 6 percent less than a year earlier. Following a 5 million pound drop in November unmanufactured tobacco exports from 1958 to 1959, July-November exports totaled 255 million pounds in 1959 compared with 272 million in 1958. Exports have been holding up fairly well although higher U. S. prices relative to foreign prices have tended to encourage increased purchases from competitors.

FATS AND OILS   Lard and tallow exports continued heavy in November. Lard exports of 71 million pounds in November 1959 were 31 million more than a year earlier. Tallow exports of 123 million pounds in November 1959 were 18 million more than in November 1958. The sharp increase in U. S. hog slaughter during the past year and lower prices have strongly stimulated lard exports while increased marketings of fatter cattle have resulted in larger tallow output available for export at competitive prices.

TRADE NEWS ROUNDUP

Although progress has been made during the past 2 years in liberalization of nontariff import restrictions against U. S. farm products, large areas of discrimination and quantitative import controls still remain. Examples: ...United Kingdom--certain fruits and fruit products, pork products (except lard and variety meats), and tobacco. ...France--grains, oilseeds and seed oils, certain fruits and vegetables, certain meat products, and tobacco. ...West Germany--grains, meat products, and certain fresh and canned deciduous fruits. ...Austria--grains and poultry. ...Italy--grains, meat products, vegetable oils, fresh and canned fruits and fruit juices, and poultry. ...Japan--lard, tallow, soybeans, raisins, and hides and skins.

————————O————————

Cuba's new economic reform policies are affecting U. S. agricultural trade with that country. Her imports of U. S. products were about the same in the first half of 1959 as in the first half of 1958 but in the third quarter dropped from $50 million to $31 million, reflecting the "buy Cuban products" campaign and a shortage of foreign exchange.

————————O————————

Japan's imports of 7 most important agricultural products in trade with U.S. amounted to $226 million during the first 9 months of 1959, down nearly one-fourth from a year earlier. Decreases occurred for wheat, barley, hides and skins, and cotton while increases took place for corn, soybeans, and tallow. Japanese imports of these products from all sources reached $572 million, up nearly 2 percent from a year earlier.

————————O————————

Japan's imports of soybeans in its fiscal year ending March 31, 1960 are expected to reach a record 40 million bushels according to revised Japanese plans. This is 29 percent more than the 31 million bushels imported in the previous year. As trade between Japan and Communist China does not appear likely to be reopened in the near future, a major part of the purchases will be made in the United States.

————————O————————

Britain's outbreaks of fowl pest this year have become more critical in the early winter months and have restricted poultry supplies available to consumers. If the epidemic worsens, Britain may buy more U. S. canned and frozen cooked chicken--items recently liberalized.

————————O————————

A fact-finding mission, consisting of specialists nominated by member countries of the Wheat Utilization Committee and FAO, is being organized to explore the possibilities of making more effective use of wheat in the Far East. The Committee, established by Food for Peace Conferences in Washington last spring, includes Argentina, Australia, Canada, France, and the United States, with FAO as observer and advisor.

Soybean export gains resumed in November after no rise in October. Soybean exports totaled 20 million bushels in November 1959, 4 million more than in November 1958. October shipments were 12 million bushels in each year. Foreign supplies have continued limited.

November shipments of cottonseed and soybean oils in 1959 were well ahead of 1958. November 1959 shipments were 98 million pounds, well above the 35 million in November 1958. July-November shipments amounted to 722 million pounds in 1959 compared with 389 million in 1958. Shipments under Title I of Public Law 480 were heavy. At the same time, exports for dollars rose sharply, probably because of a need to replenish stocks abroad and of limited supplies available from other sources.

FRUITS   Lower prices stimulated dried fruit exports. On top of an 18 million pound gain in October, combined exports of dried prunes and raisins showed a 9 million pound increase in November 1959 over 1958. July-November exports were 80 million pounds in 1958 and 65 million in 1959. Both raisins and prunes were up. The improvement reflected larger domestic supplies available to European purchasers at lower export prices.

PULSES   Excellent markets and less competition nearly doubled July-November bean exports. A 38 million pound increase in exports of dried beans in November 1959 brought the July-November export total (including USDA welfare donations) to 209 million pounds in 1959 compared with 108 million in 1958, a rise of 94 percent. Conditions were excellent in the usual Latin American markets, and there was less competition in Europe. In Latin America, Mexico took many more beans in this period due largely to the drought, and Cuba took a near record amount. At the same time, the opening of the St. Lawrence Seaway permitted a cut in freight rates which encouraged early-season sales to European buyers.

MEATS   Variety meats were the main factor in meat export gain. July-November exports of meats and meat products registered a value gain of 26 percent in 1959 over 1958, rising to $50 million. There were increases in practically all categories, but the principal ones occurred in variety meats, primarily beef and pork livers. Principal markets were in Europe.

DAIRY PRODUCTS   Lower export prices and European drought stimulated dairy product exports. July-November exports of dairy products, excluding USDA welfare donations, were valued at $53 million in 1959, one-third more than in 1958. Nearly half of the increase was due to nonfat dry milk exports, which increased sharply until mid-October under the stimulus of reduced export prices and unusually strong demand in Europe because of the drought. Although exports declined sharply from October to November following CCC's October 13 announcement to discontinue all export sales, November exports in 1959 ran 8 million pounds ahead of 1958.

POULTRY PRODUCTS   July-November poultry exports were up; shell eggs, down. Extending a sharp increase in poultry exports, shipments of all poultry meat in November 1959 were 75 percent above those of a year earlier. For July-November, these exports totaled 69 million pounds in 1959, 138 percent more than the 29 million in 1958. July-November exports

Concluded on page 8---

DOMESTIC EXPORTS: November 1958 and 1959 and July-November 1958 and 1959 a/

Commodity exported	Unit	November				July-November			
		Quantity		Value		Quantity		Value	
		1958	1959	1958	1959	1958	1959	1958	1959
		Thousands	Thousands	1,000 dollars	1,000 dollars	Thousands	Thousands	1,000 dollars	1,000 dollars
Cheese	Lb.	1,382	4,784	533	1,741	6,365	7,548	2,231	2,942
Milk, evaporated	Lb.	29,793	2,834	4,910	427	55,786	51,315	8,997	7,913
Milk, whole, dried	Lb.	3,148	2,997	1,690	1,737	10,653	11,024	5,796	6,371
Nonfat dry milk	Lb.	11,472	19,402	1,886	2,291	75,583	142,788	10,493	16,442
Eggs, in the shell	Doz.	2,209	3,848	1,130	1,643	13,369	10,043	6,256	4,980
Beef and veal, total b/	Lb.	2,161	3,117	790	1,100	10,625	13,509	3,950	4,933
Pork, total b/	Lb.	5,789	7,979	2,170	2,281	22,598	34,035	8,829	9,715
Lard	Lb.	40,352	70,722	5,407	6,497	165,915	293,746	22,376	27,225
Tallow, edible and inedible	Lb.	104,592	123,468	8,758	8,718	448,439	607,567	38,126	44,939
Cotton, unmfd, excl. linters (running bales)	Bale	314	652	45,080	77,484	1,384	1,501	191,112	175,052
Apples, fresh	Lb.	2,018	14,885	981	1,258	38,249	50,699	3,307	4,136
Oranges and tangerines, fresh	Lb.	5,695	34,871	2,189	2,447	123,714	201,750	11,707	14,612
Prunes, dried	Lb.	5,044	11,512	1,301	2,737	36,215	37,851	7,639	8,931
Raisins and currants	Lb.	12,300	13,768	3,071	2,285	28,752	42,063	6,877	7,462
Fruits, canned *	Lb.	16,872	19,080	2,602	2,689	168,411	202,866	25,496	28,085
Orange juice	Gal.	909	1,007	1,370	1,502	4,265	4,152	8,831	8,156
Barley, grn h (48 lb.)	Bu.	6,678	8,036	7,922	8,424	53,892	59,857	59,784	60,723
Corn, grain (56 lb.)	Bu.	20,453	23,340	25,806	29,421	79,479	89,173	103,481	114,921
Grain sorghums (56 lb.)	Bu.	7,715	9,253	9,814	10,384	38,103	43,734	44,835	47,955
Oats, grain (32 lb.)	Bu.	1,985	5,375	1,440	3,798	9,190	25,406	5,937	16,997
Rice, milled, excludes paddy	Lb.	61,344	108,202	5,288	7,617	618,974	745,463	47,572	49,115
Rye, grain (56 lb.)	Bu.	710	439	949	558	6,204	2,192	7,668	2,680
Wheat, grain (60 lb.)	Bu.	25,927	21,818	44,081	36,616	136,237	134,148	234,622	229,621
Flr, wholly of U. S. wheat (100 lb.)	Bag	2,233	1,925	9,251	7,449	10,625	8,986	44,464	34,924
Flaxseed (56 lb.)	Bu.	1	1,174	5	3,978	4,610	6,785	13,453	21,861
Soybeans, except canned (60 lb.)	Bu.	15,789	20,415	35,334	46,100	42,384	54,289	98,030	124,181
Soybean oil, crude, refined, etc.	Lb.	20,414	51,831	2,337	5,385	355,401	477,307	45,891	53,758
Cottonseed oil, crude, refined, etc.	Lb.	14,515	46,378	1,699	4,481	33,159	244,880	4,862	35,009
Tobacco, unmanufactured	Lb.	54,661	49,748	40,619	37,298	271,782	255,481	203,174	192,789
Beans, dried	Lb.	13,156	50,612	1,107	3,689	108,00	209,293	8,448	16,032
Peas, dried (except cowpeas and chickpeas)	Lb.	8,007	20,099	524	1,322	70,742	99,526	4,216	6,577
Potatoes, white	Lb.	21,754	13,96	471	336	136,624	127,879	3,555	3,510
Vegetables, canned *	Lb.	5,545	6,548	967	913	44,962	39,884	7,145	6,033
Food exported for relief, etc.				10,518	6,625			51,787	43,493
Other agricultural commodities				59,661	74,643			253,954	319,927
TOTAL AGRICULTURAL				341,661	405,874			1,604,901	1,752,000
ALL ALL COMMODITIES				1,581,561	1,462,370			7,300,578	7,225,179

a/ Preliminary. b/ Product weight.
* Includes only those classes which are shown separately in Table 2 of the monthly issues of "Foreign Agricultural Trade".

Compiled from official records, Bureau of the Census.

IMPORTS (FOR CONSUMPTION): October 1958 and 1959 and July-October 1958 and 1959 a/

Commodity imported	Unit	October Quantity (Thousands) 1958	1959	October Value (1,000 dollars) 1958	1959	July-October Quantity (Thousands) 1958	1959	July-October Value (1,000 dollars) 1958	1959
SUPPLEMENTARY									
Cattle, dutiable	No.	153	41	18,112	4,394	358	130	45,698	16,377
Cheese	Lb.	5,755	4,167	3,000	2,048	16,072	18,411	8,080	9,394
Hides and skins	Lb.	11,650	11,358	4,410	6,145	47,121	55,937	17,356	27,538
Beef and veal, total b/	Lb.	41,019	48,452	14,139	17,099	182,191	265,720	61,190	94,317
Pork, total b/	Lb.	15,989	11,858	10,776	7,655	62,020	51,522	42,327	33,366
Wool, unmfd., excl. free, etc. (actual weight)	Lb.	7,161	10,189	5,297	6,793	27,502	39,562	21,208	27,176
Cotton, unmfd., excl. linters (480 lb.)	Bale	12	2	1,584	185	122	124	23,304	19,598
Jute and jute butts, unmfd. (2,240 lb.)	Ton	d/	3	9	327	2	14	434	1,853
Olives in brine	Gal.	1,176	893	1,713	1,256	4,852	3,920	7,116	5,882
Pineapples, canned, prepared or preserved	Lb.	7,987	8,592	950	973	33,315	41,227	4,009	4,915
Pineapple juice	Gal.	464	352	327	273	1,579	1,370	825	758
Barley, grain (48 lb.)	Bu.	1,713	2,347	2,374	3,059	4,740	5,189	6,275	6,931
Oats, grain (32 lb.)	Bu.	195	189	177	167	2,067	646	1,624	579
Wheat, gra h (60 lb.)	Bu.	402	292	618	465	1,624	1,427	2,449	2,341
Feeds and fodders				1,391	710			4,621	2,397
Nts and preparations		2/	2/	6,870	5,873	2/	2/	22,567	26,117
Copra	Lb.	34,767	65,504	2,800	5,768	196,506	249,836	15,974	23,698
Oils, fats, ms, vegetable expressed	Lb.	47,269	43,765	8,090	7,240	196,351	178,717	31,702	31,217
Seeds, field and garden		2/	2/	1,151	1,757	2/	2/	3,719	5,735
Sugar, cane (2,000 lb.)	Ton	287	205	32,031	22,900	1,526	1,623	170,338	179,699
Molasses, unfit for human consumption	Gal.	21,020	12,190	2,131	1,256	90,123	88,781	11,044	9,222
Tobacco, cigarette leaf	Lb.	9,698	11,330	7,155	8,142	39,818	40,389	29,348	28,896
Tobacco, other	Lb.	4,435	2,810	3,143	2,536	14,288	12,255	11,398	10,383
Tomatoes, natural state	Lb.	153	482	9	28	1,693	2,870	96	193
Other supplementary									
Total supplementary				31,828	25,332			120,687	114,658
COMPLEMENTARY									
Silk, raw	Lb.	430	568	1,480	2,130	1,312	2,533	4,633	9,523
Wool, unmfd., free in bond (actual weight)	Lb.	24,930	21,362	10,816	11,227	58,034	78,230	25,917	41,501
Bananas	Bunch	4,455	4,286	5,860	5,954	15,463	17,169	21,387	23,759
Cocoa or cacao beans	Lb.	17,518	18,027	7,171	5,853	74,531	116,333	30,972	39,009
Coffee (incl. into Puerto Rico)	Lb.	271,605	194,842	109,007	65,727	823,442	1,049,997	352,862	363,692
Coffee essences, substitutes, etc.	Lb.	329	344	729	645	1,279	1,281	3,204	2,340
Tea	Lb.	8,546	9,130	3,988	4,292	32,836	34,319	15,122	15,694
Spices (complementary)	Lb.	7,670	7,325	3,046	2,793	28,731	27,673	11,712	10,733
Sisal and henequen (2,240 lb.)	Ton	13	8	1,742	1,320	37	39	4,924	6,246
Rubber, crude	Lb.	101,502	108,368	22,901	36,721	339,469	423,153	74,465	135,831
Other complementary				8,183	8,082			26,956	32,921
Total complementary				174,923	144,744			572,154	681,249
TOTAL AGRICULTURAL				335,008	277,125			1,235,543	1,364,489
TOTAL ALL COMMODITIES				1,153,274	1,214,551			4,267,610	4,989,993

a/ Preliminary. b/ Product weight. c/ Reported in value only. d/ Less than 500.

Compiled from official records, Bureau of the Census.

IMPORTS (FOR CONSUMPTION): November 1958 and 1959 and July-November 1958 and 1959 a/

Commodity imported	Unit	November Quantity (Thousands) 1958	November Quantity (Thousands) 1959	November Value (1,000 dollars) 1958	November Value (1,000 dollars) 1959	July-November Quantity (Thousands) 1958	July-November Quantity (Thousands) 1959	July-November Value (1,000 dollars) 1958	July-November Value (1,000 dollars) 1959
SUPPLEMENTARY									
Cattle, dutiable	No.	143	59	16,027	5,991	501	188	61,725	22,368
Cheese	Lb.	6,277	6,576	3,014	3,312	22,349	24,988	11,094	12,706
Hides and skins	Lb.	9,920	10,766	3,953	5,746	57,042	66,703	21,308	33,284
Beef and veal, total b/	Lb.	38,181	37,805	13,392	13,166	220,373	303,525	74,582	107,483
Pork, total b/	Lb.	16,931	11,875	10,856	7,932	78,951	63,396	53,183	41,298
Wool, unmfd., excl. free, etc. (actual weight)	Lb.	10,656	8,933	7,459	5,894	38,157	48,495	28,668	33,070
Cotton, unmfd., excl. linters (480 lb.)	Bale	d/	d/	54	25	122	124	23,358	19,623
Jute and jute butts, unmfd. (2,240 lb.)	Ton	1	5	169	842	3	20	603	2,695
Olives in brine	Gal.	994	1,202	1,542	1,722	5,846	5,122	8,658	7,604
Pineapples, canned, prepared or preserved	Lb.	4,288	5,566	475	661	37,603	46,792	4,484	5,576
Pineapple juice	Gal.	151	351	59	417	1,730	1,720	884	1,174
Barley, grain (48 lb.)	Bu.	1,402	2,563	1,950	3,306	6,143	7,753	8,225	10,236
Oats, grain (32 lb.)	Bu.	171	186	160	175	2,239	832	1,784	754
Wheat, grain (60 lb.)	Bu.	527	697	820	875	2,150	2,124	3,269	3,216
Feeds and fodders		c/	c/	1,209	702	c/	c/	5,830	3,098
Nuts and preparations		c/	c/	6,960	6,063	c/	c/	29,527	32,185
Copra	Lb.	49,159	88,552	3,993	7,923	245,665	338,388	19,967	31,621
Oils, fats, waxes, vegetable expressed	Lb.	39,618	41,138	6,877	6,763	235,970	219,855	38,579	37,980
Seeds, field and garden		c/	c/	1,393	2,079	c/	c/	5,112	7,814
Sugar, cane (2,000 lb.)	Ton	274	165	30,593	17,869	1,800	1,788	200,932	197,568
Molasses, unfit for human consumption	Gal.	36,257	15,363	3,612	1,631	126,380	104,149	14,656	10,853
Tobacco, cigarette leaf	Lb.	8,578	9,503	6,194	6,915	48,396	49,892	35,541	35,811
Tobacco, other	Lb.	3,031	3,216	2,361	2,734	17,319	15,471	13,760	13,118
Tomatoes, natural state	Lb.	3,696	3,233	39	336	2,389	8,102	135	589
Other supplementary				31,009	27,437			151,696	142,098
Total supplementary				154,170	130,581			817,560	813,822
COMPLEMENTARY									
Silk, raw	Lb.	585	726	1,971	2,826	1,897	3,259	6,604	12,349
Wool, unmfd., free in bond (actual weight)	Lb.	17,580	11,660	8,115	6,138	75,613	89,890	34,032	47,639
Bananas	Bunch	3,538	4,346	5,121	6,058	19,001	21,515	26,508	29,817
Cocoa or cacao beans	Lb.	18,904	32,230	7,533	10,236	93,435	148,562	38,506	49,244
Coffee (incl. into Puerto Rico)	Lb.	249,450	214,415	100,614	74,498	1,072,892	1,264,412	453,476	438,190
Coffee essences, substitutes, etc.	Lb.	415	414	933	803	1,693	1,695	4,130	3,143
Tea	Lb.	8,555	8,131	4,074	2,360	41,391	42,450	19,196	19,953
Spices (complementary)	Lb.	6,934	7,005	2,296	1,541	35,665	34,678	14,008	13,093
Sisal and henequen (2,240 lb.)	Ton	7	9	953	4,260	44	49	5,877	7,787
Rubber, crude	Lb.	93,674	109,411	21,985	37,206	433,143	532,564	96,450	173,037
Other complementary				6,944	7,767			33,890	40,682
Total complementary				160,539	153,693			732,693	834,941
TOTAL AGRICULTURAL				314,709	284,274			1,550,253	1,648,763
TOTAL ALL COMMODITIES				1,084,829	1,262,490			5,352,439	6,252,482

a/ Preliminary. b/ Product weight. c/ Reported in value only. d/ Less than 500.

Compiled from official records, Bureau of the Census.

of shell eggs totaled 10 million dozen in 1959 compared with 13 million in 1958. Venezuela in late 1958 took actions which restricted imports in an endeavor to stimulate its own production. Also, Canada and Denmark offered their eggs at prices more competitive than those of the United States.

IMPORT HIGHLIGHTS

Agricultural imports showed declines in November. Agricultural imports in November declined from $315 million in 1958 to $284 million in 1959. The decline in value was $23 million for supplementary (competitive) and $7 million for complementary products (items unlike those produced by U. S. agriculture). Principal reduction in the complementary group was in coffee while those in the supplementary group were in dutiable cattle and cane sugar.

July-November agricultural imports were 6 percent larger in 1959. Agricultural imports in July-November were $1,649 million in 1959, $99 million above those of a year earlier. Complementary imports increased $102 million, or 14 percent, while supplementary imports declined by $4 million, or 1 percent.

Rubber, carpet wool, and cocoa beans led in July-November complementary gain. July-November complementary imports increased from $733 million in 1958 to $834 million in 1959. Crude natural rubber, carpet wool, and cocoa beans accounted for more than 90 percent of the increase. Rubber alone accounted for 75 percent of the total complementary gain.

Beef predominated in July-November supplementary imports. July-November supplementary imports declined from $818 million in 1958 to $814 million in 1959. Beef and veal, copra, and hides and skins showed the largest advances while major reductions were in dutiable cattle and pork.

'9

FOREIGN AGRICULTURAL TRADE *Digest*

OF THE UNITED STATES

FEBRUARY 1960

Issued monthly by Foreign Agricultural Service, United States Department of Agriculture, Washington 25, D.C. Free within U.S. on request. Also available are monthly and yearly Foreign Agricultural Trade Statistical Reports, containing detailed statistics on quantity and value of exports and imports.

EXPORT HIGHLIGHTS

U. S. agricultural exports in the first half of the current fiscal year were up 12 percent. U. S. agricultural exports during the July-December period of fiscal year 1959-60 totaled $2,172 million compared with $1,941 million in the same period during the previous fiscal year. The largest percentage gains were in vegetable oils and oilseeds (+43 percent), animal products (+25 percent), vegetables and preparations (+16 percent), and cotton (+14 percent). In addition, fruits and preparations advanced 9 percent, and grains and feeds, 5 percent. The increase in grain exports, reflecting a boost of 6 percent in rice and 10 percent in feed grains, was partly offset by a reduction of 4 percent in wheat.

U.S. agricultural exports, July-December			
Commodity	1958-59 1/	1959-60	Chg.
	$ Million		%
Cotton	231	263	+14
Grains & feeds 2/	713	752	+ 5
Wheat & flour 2/	336	323	- 4
Feed grains 2/ 3/	268	296	+10
Rice, milled 2/	52	55	+ 6
Tobacco, unmfd.	240	236	- 2
Veg. oils & seeds 2/	212	304	+43
Soybeans	121	165	+36
Ed. veg. oils 2/ 4/	63	97	+54
Fruits & preps. 2/	126	137	+ 9
Vegs. & preps. 2/	63	73	+16
Animals & prods. 2/	235	293	+25
Fats & oils	75	92	+23
Meats & products	47	59	+26
Hides & skins	26	32	+23
Dairy products 2/	50	60	+20
Private relief 5/	67	52	-22
Other 2/	54	62	+15
TOTAL	1,941	2,172	+12

1/ Partly revised. 2/ Excludes private relief. 3/ Excludes products. 4/ Cottonseed and soybean. 5/ Mostly CCC donations.

December exports were 25 percent larger in 1959 than in 1958. Exports chalked up another large monthly gain this fiscal year when they mounted to $420 million in December 1959 compared with $336 million in December 1958. Cotton accounted for 58 percent of the expansion; edible vegetable oils and oilseeds, 19 percent; and grains and feeds, 18 percent.

Exports for all of fiscal year 1959-60 are now estimated at $4.2 billion. Improved prospects for exports have become sufficiently firm to warrant increasing the estimate of $4 billion made at the National Agricultural Outlook Conference last November. The increase in this estimate to $4.2 billion results mostly from better prospects for cotton, wheat, feed grains, and soybeans. This level would be the second highest in history, exceeded only by the record $4.7 billion in 1956-57 during the Suez crisis. Export value is expected to gain by 13 percent over 1958-59; and quantity, by 20 percent.

COTTON December 1959 cotton exports totaled 728 thousand bales. This brought the July-December figure to 2.2 million running bales in 1959, 29 percent ahead of the 1.7 million volume in 1958. Shipments this fiscal year are expected to total at least 6 million bales, about double the 3.1 million for 1958-59, according to revised estimates. The big up-surge reflects the competitive position pricewise of U. S. cotton in world markets, the upturn in world textile activity, and somewhat smaller avail-abilities of cotton in other exporting countries.

GRAINS AND FEEDS July-December wheat exports were little changed from a year ago. July-December wheat and flour shipments, in-cluding USDA welfare donations, were 205 million bushels in 1959 compared with 204 million in 1958. Exports for the full fiscal year are expected to reach 440 million bushels, approaching the 443 million total in 1958-59. The upward revision in the estimate results from new agreements under Title I of Public Law 480, such as that with Turkey, which were not antic-ipated earlier in the year.

Government programs have been increasing rice exports to the Far East. July-December milled rice exports, excluding USDA welfare donations, totaled 840 million pounds in 1959 compared with 674 million in 1958. This represents a gain of 25 percent, which should stretch to 40 percent for the year as a whole. Cash sales are holding up well to Cuba, Europe, and the Middle East, and a substantially expanded movement has been underway to the Far East under Title I of Public Law 480.

Feed grain exports are headed for another impressive year. July-December shipments were 6.8 million short tons in 1959 compared with 5.9 million in 1958. The year's gain will be 5 to 10 percent over 1958-59, reflecting in part the increased demand in Europe because of the drought and in large measure the growing world demand for feed grains to increase livestock production and consumption as standards of living improve. U. S. annual exports have grown by 7.5 million tons in the last 4 years.

VEGETABLE OILS Soybean exports have been especially active this fiscal AND OILSEEDS year. July-December soybean exports were 72 million bushels in 1959 compared with 53 million in 1958. Novem-ber and December 1959 shipments together totaled 38 million bushels. Seven years ago, annual exports were 30 million bushels; this fiscal year they are expected to total 130 million. Bigger exports this year have resulted largely from heavy demand for soybeans and meal, reflecting an expanding economy in Europe, drought in Europe last summer, and reduced availabili-ties from other sources.

Edible vegetable oils moved out at a record rate in July-December 1959. Shipments of soybean and cottonseed oils amounted to 797 million pounds in July-December 1959 compared with 478 million a year earlier. The im-provement stemmed from a better market in Northern Europe and from a

TRADE NEWS ROUNDUP

Foreign market opportunities for U. S. farm products and existing export promotion activities are being studied in 7 major countries in the Far East by a team of 7 State Agricultural Extension Service representatives, accompanied by USDA officials. The group left January 29 and is scheduled to return March 7 to report findings through Federal and State extension services. A similar study was made last year in Europe.

———————O———————

Foreign actions affecting U. S. farm product exports:

...France has liberalized dollar imports of natural honey, certain wines, day-old chicks, certain fatty acids, and pectin. (Dollar imports still not liberalized include poultry meat, beef, eggs, canned asparagus, peas, winter oranges, orange juice, canned and frozen fruit, lard, and state-traded items like grains, tobacco, edible oils, and oilseeds.)

...Italy has liberalized dollar imports of all live animals, butter, stone fruit, berries, dried prunes, certain minor grains, hops, pectin, and meat extracts. (Dollar imports still not liberalized include feed grains, soybeans, soybean oil, meats, honey, and canned fruit.)

...The Netherlands has liberalized dollar imports of seed rye, some rice, certain edible fats, and beet sugar.

———————O———————

Recent Title I Public Law 480 agreements announced: ...Turkey: $35 million for wheat, corn, and cottonseed and/or soybean oil. ...Israel: $30 million for wheat and/or wheat flour, feed grains, cottonseed and/or soybean oil, cotton, rice, and tobacco. ...Greece: $6 million for feed grains. ...India: $33 million for cotton. ...Uruguay: $6 million for corn and barley. ...Pakistan: $26 million for wheat. (The last three supplement earlier agreements.)

———————O———————

Market development activities carried out under Section 104(a) of Public Law 480 helped to increase U. S. poultry meat exports from 51 million pounds in 1958 to 125 million in 1959. Principal gains were in shipments to West Germany, Switzerland and the Netherlands, which increased purchases from 23 million pounds in 1958 to about 78 million in 1959. In 1955 they took less than 1 million pounds from the United States.

———————O———————

With prospects continuing favorable for an expansion in world markets for U. S. fats and oils, the Soybean Council of America has obligated over $250,000 of its funds in 1959-60 for the establishment of a 3-year, 35-nation market development agreement with FAS under Public Law 480. A number of promotional activities will be carried out to help expand foreign sales of U. S. soybeans and soybean products.

continued large movement under Public Law 480. Northern Europe's usual suppliers have smaller export availabilities this year. For the rest of 1959-60, exports will move at a reduced rate, with the year's total expected to be 1.3 billion pounds compared with 1.1 billion in 1958-59.

FRUITS AND **Both fruit and vegetable exports gained this year.** July-
VEGETABLES December shipments of fruits and preparations were $137 million in 1959, 9 percent above 1958; vegetables and preparations, at $73 million, were up 16 percent. All major fruits gained, some largely because of recent European trade liberalization. Dried beans and peas showed heavy gains. The high rate of economic activity abroad, together with European and U. S. supply conditions, underlies the current high level of U. S. exports of most fruits and vegetables.

ANIMALS AND **Exports of animals and animal products have been generally**
PRODUCTS **larger.** The overall 25 percent increase from $235 million in July-December 1958 to $293 million in July-December 1959 included advances in meats and products, fats and oils, hides and skins, and dairy products. Competitive prices for lard, tallow, poultry meat, and variety meats have greatly stimulated export sales. For the whole fiscal year, tallow and poultry meat exports are expected to set new records, and lard will be at the second highest level since World War II. The high early-year rate for dairy products may slacken, with the year's total likely to be less than in 1958-59.

IMPORT HIGHLIGHTS

Agricultural imports showed little overall change in December. U. S. agricultural imports totaled $367 million in December 1959, $2 million less than a year earlier. A $9 million decline in supplementary (competitive) imports was partly offset by a $7 million gain in complementary imports. Main value reductions in the supplementary group were in dutiable cattle, pork, and cane sugar. However, imports of beef and veal and apparel wool were larger. In the complementary group, value gains for coffee and rubber offset much of the drop in cocoa bean imports. The value rise for rubber reflected higher prices for a reduced volume.

July-December agricultural imports were up 5 percent in 1959. Agricultural imports in July-December were $2,016 million in 1959, $96 million above those of a year earlier. Complementary imports increased by $109 million, or 12 percent, while supplementary imports declined by $13 million, or 4 percent. Rubber accounted for three-fourths of the July-December value gain in complementary imports. Other complementary value increases were in silk, carpet wool, and bananas. Coffee imports declined slightly in value against a substantial rise in volume. In the supplementary group, the main value reductions were in dutiable cattle, pork, and cane sugar while the main increases were in beef and veal, hides and skins, and copra.

DOMESTIC EXPORTS: December 1958 and 1959 and July-December 1958 and 1959 a/

Commodity exported	Unit	December Quantity (Thousands) 1958	December Quantity (Thousands) 1959	December Value (1,000 dollars) 1958	December Value (1,000 dollars) 1959	July-December Quantity (Thousands) 1958	July-December Quantity (Thousands) 1959	July-December Value (1,000 dollars) 1958	July-December Value (1,000 dollars) 1959
Cheese	Lb.	953	1,845	374	704	7,318	9,393	2,605	3,646
Milk, evaporated	Lb.	19,711	4,444	3,260	634	75,497	55,759	12,257	8,547
Milk, whole, dried	Lb.	1,875	2,035	973	1,113	12,527	13,059	6,768	7,484
Nonfat dry milk	Lb.	32,366	5,550	3,383	789	107,950	148,338	13,876	17,231
Eggs, in the shell	Doz.	6,711	2,276	3,013	1,040	20,080	P, 319	9,270	6,020
Beef and veal, total b/	Lb.	2,619	2,560	1,099	1,089	13,244	16,069	5,049	6,023
Pork, total b/	Lb.	4,831	4,668	1,610	1,332	27,429	38,703	10,440	11,047
Lard	Lb.	26,129	36,585	3,444	3,460	192,044	330,331	25,820	30,685
Tallow, edible and inedible	Lb.	80,481	146,148	6,894	10,143	528,919	753,715	45,020	55,082
Cotton, unmfd., excl. linters (running bales)	Bale	298	728	39,432	87,998	1,682	2,229	230,543	263,050
Apples, fresh	Lb.	15,453	28,492	1,271	2,477	53,702	79,191	4,579	6,613
Oranges and tangerines, fresh	Lb.	36,418	40,940	2,560	2,817	160,132	242,690	14,267	17,429
Prunes, dried	Lb.	9,775	7,165	2,417	1,693	45,991	45,016	10,056	10,624
Raisins and currants	Lb.	4,205	6,381	1,119	1,020	32,957	48,444	7,996	8,482
Fruit, canned *	Lb.	14,914	13,082	2,407	1,857	183,325	215,948	27,902	29,942
Orange juice	Gal.	924	927	1,540	1,423	5,189	5,079	10,371	9,579
Barley, grain (48 lb.)	Bu.	12,406	7,510	14,585	8,339	66,298	67,367	74,369	69,062
Corn, grain (56 lb.)	Bu.	19,188	25,920	24,524	32,659	98,666	115,093	128,005	147,581
Grain sorghums (56 lb.)	Bu.	9,921	11,564	11,665	13,196	48,024	55,298	56,500	61,151
Oats, grain (32 lb.)	Bu.	2,981	1,031	2,214	830	P, 171	26,437	8,151	17,826
Rice, milled, excludes paddy	Lb.	53,810	94,378	4,599	5,903	672,785	839,841	52,171	55,018
Rye, grain (56 lb.)	Bu.	90	1,043	118	1,383	6,294	3,235	7,786	4,063
Wheat, grain (60 lb.)	Bu.	28,304	26,940	47,573	44,911	164,542	161,088	282,194	274,532
Flour, wholly of U. S. wheat (100 lb.)	Bag	2,292	3,709	8,810	13,154	12,916	P, 695	53,274	48,079
Flaxseed (56 lb.)	Bu.	44	315	157	1,073	4,654	7,100	13,610	22,934
Soybeans, except canned (60 lb.)	Bu.	10,197	18,138	23,363	40,377	52,581	72,427	121,394	164,558
Soybean oil, crude, refined, etc.	Lb.	70,140	33,238	9,539	3,484	425,541	510,545	55,430	57,242
Cottonseed oil, crude, refined, etc.	Lb.	19,378	41,418	2,263	4,598	52,537	286,298	7,125	39,607
Tobacco, unmanufactured	Lb.	48,889	57,518	36,621	43,014	320,672	312,999	239,795	235,802
Beans, dried	Lb.	17,044	25,540	1,455	2,110	125,045	234,833	9,903	18,142
Peas, dried (except cowpeas and chickpeas)	Lb.	14,868	23,120	1,002	1,549	85,609	122,646	5,218	8,126
Potatoes, white	Lb.	19,624	17,953	436	419	156,248	145,832	3,991	3,928
Vegetables, canned *	Lb.	5,485	6,522	782	1,019	50,447	46,407	7,926	7,052
Food exported for relief, etc.				15,276	8,702			67,063	52,195
Other agricultural commodities				56,333	73,664			310,288	293,591
TOTAL AGRICULTURAL				336,111	419,973			1,941,012	2,171,973
TOTAL ALL COMMODITIES				1,493,564	1,658,814			8,794,141	8,883,993

a/ Preliminary. b/ Product weight.
* Includes only those classes which are shown separately in Table 2 of the monthly issues of "Foreign Agricultural Trade".

Compiled from official records, Bureau of the Census.

IMPORTS (FOR CONSUMPTION): December 1958 and 1959 and July-December 1958 and 1959 a/

Commodity imported	Units	December Quantity (Thousand) 1958	December Quantity (Thousand) 1959	December Value (1,000 dollars) 1958	December Value (1,000 dollars) 1959	July-December Quantity (Thousand) 1958	July-December Quantity (Thousand) 1959	July-December Value (1,000 dollars) 1958	July-December Value (1,000 dollars) 1959
SUPPLEMENTARY									
Cattle, dutiable	No.	121	62	12,855	5,920	621	250	74,580	28,288
Cheese	Lb.	6,648	8,753	3,188	4,478	28,997	33,741	14,282	17,184
Hides and skins	Lb.	13,393	10,182	5,132	5,255	70,435	76,885	26,440	38,539
Beef and veal, total b/	Lb.	43,764	59,387	15,824	20,167	264,136	362,912	90,406	127,649
Pork, total b/	Lb.	18,912	13,484	11,672	9,298	97,864	76,881	64,855	50,596
Wool, unmfd., excl. free, etc. (actual weight)	Lb.	14,966	15,152	9,196	10,801	53,124	63,647	37,864	43,872
Cotton, unmfd., excl. linters (480 lb.)	Bale	1	2	75	60	123	126	23,433	19,683
Jute and jute butts, unmfd. (2,240 lb.)	Ton	3	7	710	1,391		27	1,312	4,086
Olives in brine	Gal.	806	1,475	1,234	1,936	6,652	6,597	9,893	9,539
Pineapples, canned, prepared or preserved	Lb.	4,416	4,210	511	478	42,019	51,002	4,994	6,054
Pineapple juice	Gal.	118	63	46	21	1,848	1,783	929	1,196
Barley, grain (48 lb.)	Bu.	1,768	2,176	2,316	2,766	7,911	9,928	10,541	13,003
Oats, grain (32 lb.)	Bu.	177	188	167	199	2,415	1,020	1,951	953
Wheat, grain (60 lb.)	Bu.	996	886	1,515	1,537	3,146	3,011	4,784	4,753
Feeds and fodders	c/			1,850	867			7,680	3,966
Nuts and preparations	c/			6,857	6,888			36,384	39,073
Copra	Lb.	49,707	39,560	4,200	3,818	295,372	377,948	24,167	35,439
Oils, fats, waxes, vegetable expressed	Lb.	43,210	45,296	1,376	7,616	279,179	265,151	47,001	45,596
Seeds, field and garden	c/								
Sugar, cane (2,000 lb.)	Ton	294	243	32,116	26,188	2,094	2,032	233,048	223,756
Molasses, unfit for human consumption	Gal.	24,902	17,634	3,455	2,116	151,282	121,783	18,112	12,969
Tobacco, cigarette leaf	Lb.	7,699	7,657	5,704	5,554	56,095	57,549	41,246	41,365
Tobacco, other	Lb.	2,908	2,990	2,055	2,035	20,226	18,461	15,814	15,152
Tomatoes, natural state	Lb.	6,249	26,356	432	2,248	8,638	34,459	567	2,837
Other supplementary				34,286	32,127			185,983	174,224
Total supplementary				165,194	156,407			982,754	970,229
COMPLEMENTARY									
Silk, raw	Lb.	737	729	2,344	3,017	2,634	3,987	8,948	15,366
Wool, unmfd., free in bond (actual weight)	Lb.	19,280	13,825	8,801	7,346	94,893	103,715	42,832	54,986
Bananas	Bunch	4,028	4,666	6,004	7,088	23,029	26,181	32,511	36,905
Cocoa or cacao beans	Lb.	92,266	73,593	34,050	23,026	185,701	222,155	72,556	72,270
Coffee (incl. into Puerto Rico)	Lb.	268,678	313,359	103,525	113,286	1,341,570	1,577,771	557,001	551,476
Coffee essences, substitutes, etc.	Lb.	432	524	950	915	2,125	2,220	5,087	4,058
Tea	Lb.	11,121	11,042	5,255	5,590	52,513	53,492	24,451	25,544
Spices (complementary)	Lb.	6,594	8,152	2,552	2,745	42,259	42,830	16,560	15,838
Sisal and henequen (2,240 lb.)	Ton	12	10	1,723	1,709	56	58	7,600	9,496
Rubber, crude	Lb.	122,063	106,273	30,808	35,690	555,206	638,837	127,259	208,726
Other complementary				8,160	10,409			42,059	51,097
Total complementary				204,172	210,821			936,864	1,045,762
TOTAL AGRICULTURAL				369,366	367,228			1,919,618	2,015,991
TOTAL ALL COMMODITIES				1,229,094	1,431,555			6,581,534	7,684,038

a/ Preliminary. b/ Product weight. c/ Reported in value only.

Compiled from official records, Bureau of the Census.

UNITED STATES DEPARTMENT OF AGRICULTURE
WASHINGTON 25, D. C.

Official Business

FOREIGN AGRICULTURAL TRADE

Digest

OF THE UNITED STATES

MARCH 1960

Issued monthly by Foreign Agricultural Service, United States Department of Agriculture, Washington 25, D.C. Free within U.S. on request. Also available are monthly and yearly Foreign Agricultural Trade Statistical Reports, containing detailed statistics on quantity and value of exports and imports.

EXPORT HIGHLIGHTS

July-January agricultural exports in 1959-60 were 15 percent ahead of 1958-59.
July-January agricultural exports totaled $2,585 million in 1959-60, compared with $2,252 million in 1958-59. Over 60 percent of the gain was in cotton ($140 million), soybeans ($45 million), and animal products ($37 million); but increases were also registered in edible vegetable oils, feed grains, fruits, vegetables, and rice. Tobacco exports were close to the 1958-59 level.

U. S. agricultural exports, July-January

Commodity	1958-59	1959-60	Chg.
	Million dollars		%
Cotton	260	400	+54
Grains & feeds 1/	889	924	+4
Wheat & flour 1/	435	424	-3
Feed grains 1/ 2/	319	336	+5
Rice, milled 1/	60	66	+10
Tobacco, unmfd.	260	253	-3
Veg. oils & seeds	251	340	+35
Soybeans	143	188	+31
Ed. veg. oils 3/	77	107	+39
Fruits & preps.	140	156	+11
Vegs. & preps. 1/	72	86	+19
Animals & prods. 1/	313	350	+12
Fats & oils	90	109	+21
Meats & prods.	56	67	+20
Hides & skins	30	38	+27
Dairy products 1/	92	79	-14
Other 1/	67	76	+13
TOTAL	2,252	2,585	+15

1/ Includes private relief, starting with March 1960 issue. 2/ Excludes products. 3/ Cottonseed and soybean.

January exports were a third larger in 1960. January exports totaled $413 million in 1960, up 33 percent over the $310 million of 1959. The principal gains occurred in cotton and soybeans; and the main declines were in feed grains and edible vegetable oils. Cotton exports expanded by $108 million.

Exports to the 5 largest markets in July-December increased by 21 percent. July-December exports to the 5 principal overseas markets for U. S. farm products--the United Kingdom, Canada, the Netherlands, Japan, and West Germany (in that order)--increased from $847 million in fiscal year 1958-59 to $1,028 million in 1959-60. This gain accounted for over three-fourths of the total rise of $231 million. The largest export gain was $75 million to the Netherlands; other major advances were $42 million to Egypt, $32 million each to Canada and West

Germany, and $26 million to the United Kingdom. Major reductions occurred in exports to India, Cuba, and Mexico.

COTTON January cotton exports surged to highest level in a quarter
century. January 1960 cotton exports, excluding linters, totaled 1,109 thousand running bales, almost 900 thousand more than in 1959 and the largest volume since November 1935. July-January exports amounted to 3,338 thousand bales in 1959-60, 75 percent larger than the 1,904 thousand in 1958-59. The improvement reflects competitive U. S. prices, increased foreign consumption, and reduced foreign production and beginning stocks. More U. S. cotton has moved to Western Europe, Canada, and Japan.

GRAINS AND FEEDS Feed grain and rice exports remained ahead of 1958-59;
wheat shipments, about the same. July-January wheat and flour shipments, including USDA welfare donations, were 246 million bushels in 1959-60, 1 percent less than the 248 million in 1958-59. This fiscal year, more wheat and flour have moved out under the Title I Public Law 480 and USDA donation programs, but dollar sales were below those of a year earlier.

Feed grain exports in the July-January period totaled 7.7 million short tons in 1959-60 compared with 7 million in 1958-59. The higher volume of exports this year reflects the expanding livestock industry in Europe and last summer's drought there. However, January exports totaled 880 thousand tons in 1960, 233 thousand less than in January 1959, and 366 thousand less than in December 1959. With the exception of oats, prices of feed grains this year have been slightly below those of a year earlier. Feed grain shipments to Europe slowed somewhat in January 1960 due to congestion of grain facilities at Rotterdam, the largest receiving terminal for U. S. grains in Europe. In addition, U. S. exports encountered increased competition from Mexico's larger corn exports from its record 1959 crop.

U. S. agricultural exports by country of destination, July-December 1958 and 1959

Country	1958	1959	Chg.
	Million dollars		%
United Kingdom	239.2	264.9	+11
Canada	174.3	205.7	+18
The Netherlands	120.1	195.1	+62
Japan	165.0	182.1	+10
West Germany	148.3	180.0	+21
Italy	62.5	73.6	+18
Belgium	51.0	69.7	+14
Cuba	77.8	65.7	-16
India	107.2	64.5	-40
Egypt	7.9	49.7	+529
Venezuela	46.9	49.1	+5
Poland	44.0	46.1	+5
France	45.5	43.0	-6
Brazil	32.7	42.0	+28
Denmark	22.6	37.7	+67
Mexico	44.4	33.2	-25
Other	551.6	569.9	+3
TOTAL	1,941.0	2,172.0	+12

July-January milled rice exports, amounting to 1,014 million pounds this fiscal year, were 29 percent larger than a year ago. This gain reflects the improved competitive position of U. S. rice in world markets as well as the larger shipments under Title I of Public Law 480 this year.

Continued on page 4 . . . . .

TRADE NEWS ROUNDUP

U. S. tobacco exporters expect to derive immediate benefits from Britain's announcement that restrictions are being lifted on dollar imports of unmanufactured tobacco and manufactured tobacco products (except cigars). Several British manufacturers have low stocks of U. S. leaf; and, if the 1960 U. S. crop is suitable, this should encourage larger U. K. purchases. British tobacco firms, however, still have discriminatory guaranteed-purchase agreements with Rhodesia and Nyasaland, and Commonwealth producing countries enjoy a tariff preference of about 21½ cents a pound.

———————O———————

Colombia may again become an important market for U. S. breeding cattle. The recent removal of its ban on breeding-cattle imports has been followed by a reduction of import duties. Before Colombia restricted imports in 1957 under a foreign trade austerity program, it had taken nearly 5 thousand U. S. animals annually in 1954 and 1955.

———————O———————

Recent Title I Public Law 480 agreements announced: ...Poland: $42 million for wheat. ...Peru: $12 million for wheat, edible fats and oils, and rice. ...Taiwan: $6 million for wheat and/or wheat flour. ...Viet Nam: $1 million for cotton. (Agreements with Poland and Taiwan supplement earlier ones.)

———————O———————

Canada is the latest of several countries to remove embargoes on imports of U. S. hogs and pork imposed because of the previous existence of vesicular exanthema in several States. Canadian importers had been notified in December 1959 that the United States is now free of this disease.

———————O———————

A recent example of effective foreign market development work is provided by the Great Plains Wheat Growers Association. This organization financed a U. S. visit of wheat buyers from two important British flour mills, resulting in a resumption of monthly purchases of 2 million bushels of hard red winter wheat.

———————O———————

Under Cuba's trade agreement with the USSR--signed February 13--the USSR has agreed to buy 1.1 million short tons of sugar annually for 5 years. (Cuban sales to the USSR have averaged 300 thousand tons in recent years.) The USSR will pay for this sugar partly with industrial equipment, petroleum, wheat, and chemicals along with technical assistance. Cuba is aiming at a 1960 sugar crop of 6¼ million tons, more than enough to enable it to meet its U. S. quota of 3.1 million tons for 1960 and to fulfill its agreement with the USSR.

———————O———————

VEGETABLE OILS July-January exports of vegetable oils and oilseeds were
AND OILSEEDS   up nearly $90 million in 1959-60. Exports of these com-
                modities totaled $340 million in July-January 1959-60,
35 percent larger than the $251 million a year earlier. Soybeans alone
accounted for one-half of the total increase. Vegetable oil exports were
highlighted by a 4-fold volume increase in cottonseed oil while soybean
oil exports gained slightly over a year earlier. The overall increase for
this group reflects reduced availabilities from other major suppliers,
last summer's drought in Europe, and higher consumption in the industrialized countries. Most of the export expansion in vegetable oil was in
dollar sales as shipments under Government programs were about the same in
both years.

FRUITS AND   Fruit and vegetable exports continued at high levels. July-
VEGETABLES   January exports of fruits and preparations totaled $156 mil-
              lion in 1959-60, 11 percent more than in 1958-59; and those
of vegetables and preparations totaled $86 million, 19 percent greater
than in 1958-59. There were increases in fresh oranges, apples, and
pears and in canned fruits. Among the vegetables, expanded shipments of
beans and peas resulted from short supplies in both Europe and Latin
America. The competitive position of U. S. dry edible beans in Europe
this year was improved by the opening of the St. Lawrence Seaway; the
beans moved sooner and at lower transportation costs than a year earlier.

ANIMALS AND   Exports of all major animal products were up. Shipments
ANIMAL PRODUCTS of animals and animal products in July-January 1959-60
                 totaled $350 million, 12 percent above the $313 million
in 1958-59. Shipments of lard, tallow, poultry meats, and variety meats
gained substantially, reflecting plentiful U. S. supplies coupled with
competitive prices. Although USDA foreign donations of dairy products
were considerably below those of a year ago, commercial exports were up
18 percent for the first 7 months in 1959-60. Large amounts of nonfat
dry milk and butter were exported to Europe to supplement its deficit
this fiscal year. The July-January increase in the export value of hides
and skins represents higher prices this season as the quantity shipped
was below the 1958-59 level.

                    I M P O R T   H I G H L I G H T S

January agricultural imports were 18 percent less in value this year.
January's agricultural imports of $270 million in 1960 compared with $328
million in 1959. Imports were smaller for both major classes: Supplementary (competitive) products and complementary (noncompetitive) products.
The bulk of the decline in January resulted from reduced imports of coffee,
rubber, and cocoa beans.

July-January imports ran 2 percent ahead of a year ago. July-January's
$2,285 million in 1959-60 compared with $2,248 million in 1958-59. For
the 7-month period, complementary imports were larger by $69 million while
supplementary imports were smaller by $32 million.

Seven-month complementary imports registered 6-percent gain over 1958-59.
Imports of complementary products rose from $1,104 million in 1958-59 to

$1,173 million in 1959-60. Rubber increased most in value, but other gainers included carpet wool, raw silk, bananas, tea, and sisal and henequen. The increase in carpet wool reflected only higher prices as the quantity imported was practically unchanged from 1958-59. A substantial decline occurred in the value of coffee imports, but it represented lower prices as the quantity brought in was up almost 200 million pounds.

Supplementary imports in the July-January period were down by 3 percent from year-ago level. Supplementary imports in the July-January period declined from $1,144 million in 1958-59 to $1,112 million in 1959-60. Largest single decline was in dutiable cattle; other losers included pork, cotton, feeds and fodders, vegetable oils and waxes, cane sugar, and molasses unfit for human consumption. The reduction in value for cotton reflected lower prices as the quantity imported increased. Biggest value increase among supplementary items was in beef and veal; other gainers included hides and skins, cheese, mutton, apparel wool, jute, canned pineapples, feed grains, copra, field and garden seeds, and fresh tomatoes. The rise in value for hides and skins was due more to higher prices than to a gain in quantity.

DOMESTIC EXPORTS: January 1959 and 1960 and July-January 1958-59 and 1959-60 1/

Commodity exported	Unit	January Quantity (Thousands) 1959	1960	January Value 2/ (1,000 dollars) 1959	1960	July-January Quantity (Thousands) 1958-59	1959-60	July-January Value 2/ (1,000 dollars) 1958-59	1959-60
Evaporated milk*	Lb.	940	1,353	409	501	46,957	10,842	12,914	4,172
Dried whole milk*	Lb.	5,057	5,840	788	921	80,609	61,665	13,053	9,486
Nonfat dry milk*	Lb.	3,961	1,981	1,411	1,155	16,488	15,040	8,179	8,640
Eggs, in the shell	Doz.	40,771	20,906	4,531	2,605	374,042	308,042	42,457	32,272
Hides and skins 3/	No.	2,380	1,194	1,371	781	22,460	13,514	10,641	6,801
Beef and veal, total 4/	Lb.	635	630	3,882	5,056	5,014	4,449	29,564	38,217
Pork, total 4/	Lb.	1,919	2,494	833	1,072	15,163	18,532	5,882	7,082
Variety meats 5/	Lb.	4,976	4,849	1,528	1,476	32,405	43,552	11,968	12,522
Poultry, canned, fresh or frozen 4/	Lb.	8,250	11,085	1,954	2,121	50,578	60,946	12,233	12,045
Lard	Lb.	8,564	9,430	2,657	2,375	43,723	88,958	4,007	24,261
Tallow, edible and inedible	Lb.	42,149	68,800	5,047	6,176	234,193	399,131	30,867	36,860
Cotton, unmfd., excl. linters (running bales)	Bale	12,940	138,449	29,278	136,906	64,859	892,164	259,822	399,813
Apples, fresh	Lb.	18,460	39,638	1,464	2,731	72,162	284,471	6,042	9,880
Oranges and tangerines, fresh	Lb.	39,532	41,781	2,366	2,180	199,664	18,829	16,633	20,161
Prunes, dried	Lb.	2,984	9,224	821	1,125	48,975	54,240	10,878	12,804
Raisins and currants	Lb.	2,749	7,331	763	2,239	35,706	55,775	8,759	9,606
Fruits, canned 6/	Lb.	8,101	15,222	1,360	2,085	191,426	231,170	29,262	32,181
Orange juice 6/	Gal.	1,232	1,579	2,022	2,085	6,421	6,657	2,398	11,664
Barley, grain (48 lb.)	Bu.	10,754	8,114	13,039	9,497	77,097	75,481	87,484	78,558
Corn, grain (56 lb.)*	Bu.	16,399	13,656	21,535	17,818	115,750	128,954	150,623	165,737
Grain sorghums (56 lb.)	Bu.	11,576	8,870	14,216	9,835	59,600	64,168	70,362	70,986
Oats, grain (32 lb.)	Bu.	3,902	3,398	2,818	3,128	16,073	29,835	10,968	20,954
Rice, milled, excludes paddy*	Lb.	80,202	170,432	6,009	10,349	787,457	1,014,440	60,150	65,640
Rye, grain (56 lb.)	Bu.	304	474	412	597	6,598	3,709	8,198	4,661
Wheat, grain (60 lb.)*	Bu.	35,150	33,797	60,344	57,562	200,539	195,411	344,116	333,327
Flour, wholly of U. S. wheat (100 lb.)*	Bag	3,311	3,176	14,815	11,870	20,205	21,893	91,221	90,897
Oil cake and oil-cake meal (2,000 lb.)*	Ton	60	94	3,872	6,338	281	649	18,093	42,380
Flaxseed (56 lb.)	Bu.	224	9	746	39	4,878	7,109	14,355	22,973
Soybeans, except canned (60 lb.)	Bu.	9,316	10,263	21,517	23,131	61,896	82,690	142,911	187,689
Soybean oil, crude, refined, etc.	Lb.	88,152	30,888	10,886	3,146	513,692	541,433	66,315	60,388
Cottonseed oil, crude, refined, etc.	Lb.	31,160	65,798	3,451	6,788	83,697	352,091		46,392
Tobacco, unmanufactured	Lb.	27,469	23,072	20,123	16,927	348,140	336,071	259,918	252,730
Beans, dried*	Lb.	18,410	35,197	1,529	2,930	144,112	270,826	11,480	21,101
Peas, dried (except cowpeas and chickpeas)	Lb.	12,270	20,010	825	1,231	97,880	142,656	6,043	9,357
Potatoes, white	Lb.	23,584	19,539	528	544	179,832	165,371	4,519	4,472
Vegetables, canned 6/	Lb.	4,882	7,742	708	1,160	55,329	54,149	8,634	8,213
Other agricultural commodities				40,618	46,072			295,850	345,727
TOTAL AGRICULTURAL COMMODITIES				309,989	413,196			2,251,903	2,585,292
TOTAL NONAGRICULTURAL COMMODITIES				1,074,799	1,129,073			7,927,027	7,840,970
TOTAL ALL COMMODITIES				1,384,788	1,542,269			10,178,930	10,426,262

1/ Preliminary. 2/ At place of export. 3/ Excludes the weight of "other hides and skins", reported in value only. 4/ Product weight. 5/ Includes beef and pork livers, beef tongues, and other variety meats, fresh or frozen. Product weight. 6/ Includes only classes shown separately in Table 2 of the monthly "Foreign Agricultural Trade".
* Includes "Food exported for relief or charity by individuals and private agencies".

Compiled from official records, Bureau of the Census.

IMPORTS (FOR CONSUMPTION): January 1959 and 1960 and July-January 1958-59 and 1959-60 1/

Commodity Imported	Unit	Quantity January 1959	Quantity January 1960	Value January 1959	Value January 1960	Quantity July-January 1958-59	Quantity July-January 1959-60	Value July-January 1958-59	Value July-January 1959-60
		Thousands	Thousands	1,000 dollars	1,000 dollars	Thousands	Thousands	1,000 dollars	1,000 dollars
SUPPLEMENTARY									
Cattle, dutiable	No.	85	46	9,364	4,421	706	296	83,944	32,709
Casein or lactarene	Lb.	7,993	5,981	1,533	1,244	52,890	47,340	10,042	9,273
Cheese	Lb.	5,320	4,167	2,406	1,853	34,318	37,908	16,688	19,037
Hides and skins	Lb.	14,596	9,688	6,292	5,268	85,031	86,573	32,733	43,807
Beef and veal, total 2/	Lb.	42,574	39,345	15,954	13,328	306,710	402,257	106,360	140,478
Pork, total 2/	Lb.	18,404	15,057	12,293	10,244	116,268	91,938	7,148	60,840
Mutton, goat and lamb, fresh or frozen 2/	Lb.	4,551	5,888	1,178	1,233	17,333	30,513	4,309	6,671
Sausage casings	Lb.	1,186	1,238	815	853	9,104	8,669	7,554	6,193
Wool, unmfd., e cxl free, etc. (actual weight)	Lb.	15,781	13,514	9,690	9,504	68,905	77,062	47,554	53,306
Cotton, unmfd., excl. interi (480 lb.)	Bale	1	2	100	241	124	128	23,533	19,924
Jute and jute butts, unmfd. (2,240 lb.)	Ton	7	10	1,363	1,705	13	37	2,675	5,791
Olives in brine	Gal.	1,021	1,100	1,601	1,385	7,674	7,697	11,493	10,925
Pineapples, canned, prepared or preserved	Lb.	3,410	10,789	361	1,144	45,429	61,791	5,355	7,199
Barley, grain (48 lb.)	Bu.	341	395	386	543	8,252	10,326	10,927	13,548
Oats, grain (32 lb.)	Bu.	116	1	122	124	2,531	1,131	2,073	1,077
Wheat, grain (60 lb.)	Bu.	642	711	1,108	1,162	3,788	3,722	5,892	5,915
Feeds and fodders		3/	3/	1,645	692	3/	3/	9,325	4,658
Nuts and preparations				6,904	4,420			43,288	43,493
Copra	Lb.	53,799	40,338	5,027	3,750	349,171	418,286	29,194	39,189
Vegetable oils, fats, and waxes, expressed	Lb.	35, 2	33,660	6,726	6,160	314,401	298,746	53,727	51,712
Seeds, field and garden		3/	3/	1,239	2,086	3/	3/	7,727	12,546
Sugar, cane (2,000 lb.)	Ton	324	315	35,888	32,209	2,418	2,350	268,935	256,375
Molasses, unfit for human consumption	Gal.	19,050	16,461	2,202	1,591	170,331	138,244	20,314	14,560
Tobacco, unmanufactured	Lb.	13,624	14,675	9,974	10,013	89,945	90,643	67,034	66,505
Tomatoes, natural state	Lb.	26,549	49,250	1,938	4,070	35,187	83,708	24,506	66,908
Other supplementary				25,636	22,923			194,168	179,528
Total supplementary				161,745	142,166			1,144,498	1,112,167
COMPLEMENTARY									
Silk, raw	Lb.	416	561	1,352	2,348	3,051	4,549	10,300	17,713
Wool, unmfd., free in bond (actual weight)	Lb.	25,583	16,281	11,567	8,826	120,476	120,096	54,399	63,881
Bananas	Bunch	3,645	4,053	5,632	5,495	26,673	30,234	38,143	42,400
Cocoa or co beans	Lb.	49,888	32,280	18,324	9,541	235,589	254,435	90,880	81,811
Coffee (incl. into Puerto Rico)	Lb.	210,078	163,456	79,642	56,784	1,551,648	1,741,696	636,643	608,058
Coffee essences, substitutes, etc.	Lb.	274	382	524	634	2,399	2,601	5,611	4,692
Tea	Lb.	8,498	9,644	4,054	4,722	61,010	63,136	28,505	30,266
Spices (complementary)	Lb.	8,493	7,698	3,086	3,059	50,752	50,528	19,645	18,897
Abaca or Manila (2,240 lb.)	Ton	2	2	804	957	27	19	8,539	8,649
Sisal and heneqûen (2,240 lb.)	Ton	10	10	1,928	1,790	66	69	9,528	11,286
Rubber, crude	Lb.	123,088	77,941	32,654	26,858	678,294	716,722	159,913	234,502
Other complementary				2,076	7,147			41,402	50,552
Total complementary				166,643	128,161			1,103,508	1,172,707
TOTAL AGRICULTURAL COMMODITIES				328,388	270,327			2,248,006	2,284,874
TOTAL NONAGRICULTURAL COMMODITIES				806,134	891,887			5,468,049	6,561,378
TOTAL ALL COMMODITIES				1,134,522	1,162,214			7,716,055	8,846,252

1/ Preliminary.   2/ Product weight.   3/ Reported in value only.

Compiled from official records, Bureau of the Census.

UNITED STATES DEPARTMENT OF AGRICULTURE
WASHINGTON 25, D. C.
———
Official Business

FOREIGN AGRICULTURAL TRADE

Digest

OF THE UNITED STATES

APRIL 1960

Issued monthly by Foreign Agricultural Service, United States Department of Agriculture, Washington 25, D.C. Free within U.S. on request. Also available are monthly and yearly Foreign Agricultural Trade Statistical Reports, containing detailed statistics on quantity and value of exports and imports.

EXPORT HIGHLIGHTS

July-February agricultural exports were 19 percent larger this year. July-February agricultural exports were $2,984 million in 1959-60 compared with $2,501 million in 1958-59. Principal value gains were in cotton ($220 million), soybeans ($43 million), cottonseed oil ($43 million), animal fats ($21 million), fruits and preparations ($21 million), and rice ($15 million). Other increases occurred in feed grains, vegetables and preparations, meats, and wheat. Tobacco exports were at the level of 1958-59.

February exports were three-fifths larger this year. Exports this February of $399 million were 60 percent larger than February 1959's $250 million. Over half of the increase was accounted for by cotton. Other substantial gains were in wheat, vegetable oils, rice, tobacco, and fruits and preparations. Exports of animals and animal products, feed grains, soybeans, and vegetables and preparations were about the same as in February 1959.

Fiscal year 1959-60 exports are now estimated at $4.5 billion. With further export gains in sight for cotton, wheat, vegetable oils, and animal products, the estimate for this fiscal year's agricultural exports has been raised to $4.5 billion. This is $500 million above the original estimate made at the time of the National Agricultural Outlook Conference last November and $800 million above actual exports in 1958-59. This level of exports would be exceeded only by the record $4.7 billion in

U. S. agricultural exports, July-February

Commodity	1958-59	1959-60	Chg.
	Million dollars		%
Cotton	286	506	+77
Grains & feeds 1/	1,004	1,076	+7
Wheat & flour 1/	494	507	+3
Feed grains 1/ 2/	362	381	+5
Rice, milled 1/	65	80	+23
Tobacco, unmfd.	272	272	0
Veg. oils & seeds	277	375	+35
Soybeans	162	205	+27
Ed. veg. oils 3/	80	121	+51
Fruits & preps.	154	175	+14
Vegs. & preps. 1/	82	97	+18
Animals & prods. 1/	349	394	+13
Fats & oils	103	124	+20
Meats & prods.	62	76	+23
Hides & skins	34	46	+35
Dairy products 1/	99	88	-11
Other 1/	77	89	+16
TOTAL	2,501	2,984	+19

1/ Includes private relief, starting with March 1960 issue. 2/ Excludes products. 3/ Cottonseed and soybean.

1956-57 during the Suez crisis. This year's latest value estimate is one-fifth larger than actual exports in 1958-59 while the quantity is expected to rise even more.

COTTON   Cotton exports in fiscal year 1959-60 are now expected to be about 6.5 million bales. July-February cotton exports, excluding lint-ers, of 4,177 thousand running bales were almost double those of a year earlier. Although exports of 839 thousand bales in February 1960 were 24 percent below the large January shipments of 1,109 thousand, they were about 4 times the February 1959 level of 211 thousand bales. Larger U. S. exports this year reflect (1) rising consumption in most major importing countries following the 1958 textile recession, (2) ample supplies of U. S. cotton at competitive prices, and (3) smaller exportable supplies in major foreign producing countries.

GRAINS AND FEEDS   Wheat exports may reach 475 million bushels this fiscal year. July-February wheat and flour exports, including USDA welfare donations, were 295 million bushels in 1959-60, 5 percent more than the 282 million in 1958-59. February 1960 exports of 49 million bushels were 15 million larger than in February 1959. Wheat exports in fiscal year 1959-60 are expected to exceed the 443 million bushels shipped in 1958-59 with prospects of reaching 475 million bushels. The improved outlook for wheat stems mostly from increased movements under Title I of Public Law 480 and larger USDA donations under Title III of Public Law 480. Commercial sales for dollars may be somewhat below those of the previous year, reflecting largely an increased supply situation in Europe.

July-February feed grain exports were 10 percent larger than a year ago. July-February exports reached 8.7 million short tons this year as compared with 7.9 million last year. February 1960 exports of 963 thousand tons were 53 thousand larger than in February a year ago and 83 thousand larger than in January 1960. Exports for fiscal year 1959-60 are forecast at 13.1 million short tons, 10 percent greater than the 1958-59 level. Seven-tenths of U. S. feed grain exports in July-February went to Western Europe to supplement reduced forage output following last summer's drought and to meet increased feed requirements of the expanding livestock industry. Most of the increase occurred before December 1959. December-February exports to Europe moved at a reduced rate in response to a large buildup of feed grain stocks while exports to other areas increased. For the remainder of the year, however, exports to Europe are expected to improve.

Rice exports showed 45-percent gain in July-February. Milled rice exports in July-February this fiscal year totaled 12,263 thousand bags as compared with 8,466 thousand in 1958-59. February shipments of 2,118 thousand bags in 1960 were 1,527 thousand larger than in 1959. Plentiful U. S. supplies and competitive prices were major factors in this year's gain. Nearly one-half moved under Title I of Public Law 480.

VEGETABLE OILS   July-February exports of vegetable oils and oilseeds were
AND OILSEEDS   up 35 percent. Exports of vegetable oils and oilseeds
                 totaled $375 million in July-February of 1959-60, $98 mil-
lion greater than in the same period last year. Soybean exports of 90 million bushels this year were 20 million more than in 1958-59. Cottonseed

TRADE NEWS ROUNDUP

USDA is conducting an overall review of current export policies, programs, and activities as a basis for further expanding its agricultural trade promotion activities, as called for by the President in his March 17 message to the Congress on the National Export Expansion Program. The review includes such elements as trade barrier removal, quality, credit, pricing, promotion activities of Government and industry, and Government-financed exports under the "Food for Peace" concept.

———————O———————

Foreign market opportunities for U. S. farm products and existing export promotion activities are being studied in 7 Latin American countries by a Federal and State Extension Service team. The team is scheduled to return May 26 to report findings through Federal and State Extension Services. Similar studies have been made in Europe and the Far East.

———————O———————

Looking ahead to further dollar-trade liberalization, the United States has scheduled consultations during the remainder of 1960 with 24 member countries of the General Agreement on Tariffs and Trade to discuss removal of import restrictions against U. S. commodities for balance-of-payments reasons.

———————O———————

The sale of $168 thousand worth of U. S. Brown Swiss and Holstein breeding stock at the agricultural fair in Verona, Italy, March 13-20, is an indication that Italy not only offers a good potential market for feed grains but is an actual market for quality dairy cattle as well. Italy recently liberalized dollar imports of live animals, including poultry.

———————O———————

USDA announced on March 16 that the payment-in-kind export program for cotton--in effect since the start of the 1958-59 marketing year--will be continued in the 1960-61 year. The initial rate of export payment for cotton shipped on or after August 1, 1960 will be 6 cents a pound as compared with 8 cents under the current program.

———————O———————

Title I Public Law 480 agreements signed since mid-March: India (Supplemental): $7.8 million for rice. Finland: $4.6 million for tobacco, cotton, raisins, and canned fruit. UAR-Egypt: $15 million for tobacco, cottonseed oil or soybean oil, and corn. Iceland: $1.8 million for wheat or wheat flour, cracked corn or cornmeal, rice, barley or barley meal, tobacco or tobacco products, and cottonseed oil or soybean oil. Pakistan (New): $72 million for wheat or wheat flour to be shipped over 2-year period. (Supplemental): $16 million for cottonseed oil or soybean oil, extra-long staple cotton, and tobacco.

———————O———————

oil exports were 3 times larger this year. Supplies of oilseeds and vegetable oils from other major producers have remained tight this fiscal year.
Also, the demand for U. S. vegetable oils and oilseeds in Europe has been
strong because of the increasingly higher living standards. At the same
time, oilseed and meal exports to Europe have been encouraged by last season's drought. Commercial sales for dollars have accounted for the increase
in vegetable oil exports this year as exports under Government programs
have been about the same as in fiscal year 1958-59.

FRUITS AND   Both fruit and vegetable exports were larger in July-February
VEGETABLES   of 1959-60. July-February exports of fruits and preparations
                totaled $175 million in 1959-60, 14 percent more than in
1958-59; and those of vegetables and preparations totaled $97 million, 18
percent greater. The quantity of fresh oranges exported was up 36 percent,
apples 70 percent, and major canned fruits 19 percent. Fruit exports this
year have benefited from trade liberalization in Western Europe in the past
year. The larger vegetable exports were accounted for by dry beans and
peas shipped to Latin America and Europe. Exports of dry edible beans to
Europe are expected to increase substantially in the remainder of this
fiscal year with the reopening of the St. Lawrence Seaway.

ANIMALS AND   Exports of all major animal products except dairy products
ANIMAL PRODUCTS   were up in July-February of 1959-60. July-February ex-
                   ports of animals and animal products, including USDA dona-
tions, totaled $394 million in 1959-60, 13 percent more than the $349 million in 1958-59. Exports of lard, tallow, poultry meats, and variety meats
have been stimulated this year by plentiful U. S. supplies and relatively
low prices. While July-February total exports of dairy products were below
those of a year earlier, exports excluding USDA donations were 21 percent
greater this year. Exports of nonfat dry milk are expected to expand during
the March-June period as CCC supplies have once more been made available
under the USDA donation program.

IMPORT HIGHLIGHTS

July-February agricultural imports were 2 percent ahead this year, reflecting increases in noncompetitive products. Agricultural imports totaled
$2,628 million in the first 8 months of this fiscal year compared with the
$2,582 million a year earlier. Supplementary imports of $1,269 million
were 2 percent less than the $1,297 million in 1958-59. There were value
declines in dutiable cattle ($52 million), pork ($15 million), and cane
sugar ($8 million). These declines were partially offset by gains in beef
and veal, hides and skins, copra, and fresh tomatoes. Complementary imports of $1,359 million were 6 percent larger than the $1,285 million in
1958-59. The most significant increase in this group was the $78 million
gain in rubber. Other value gains were in silk, carpet wool, bananas,
spices, sisal and henequen, and tea. The quantity of coffee was 173 million pounds greater, but value was $35 million less. Imports of cocoa
beans were 25 million pounds larger in volume but $10 million smaller in
value.

Agricultural imports were up slightly in February. Imports totaled $343
million in February 1960 compared with the $334 million in February 1959.

Both supplementary (somewhat competitive) and complementary (noncompetitive) products were 3 percent larger. Principal supplementary value gains were in cane sugar, fresh tomatoes, pork, tobacco, and copra. There were declines in beef and veal, hides and skins, cattle, and vegetable oils. Principal complementary gains were in spices and rubber while declines occurred in coffee and cocoa beans.

DOMESTIC EXPORTS: February 1959 and 1960 and July-February 1958-59 and 1959-60 1/

Commodity exported	Unit	February Quantity 1959 (Thousands)	February Quantity 1960 (Thousands)	February Value 2/ 1959 (1,000 dollars)	February Value 2/ 1960 (1,000 dollars)	July-February Quantity 1958-59 (Thousands)	July-February Quantity 1959-60 (Thousands)	July-February Value 2/ 1958-59 (1,000 dollars)	July-February Value 2/ 1959-60 (1,000 dollars)
Cheese*	Lb.	902	911	307	383	47,859	11,752	13,220	4,556
Evaporated milk*	Lb.	2,083	5,941	296	970	82,692	67,605	13,349	10,456
Dried whole milk	Lb.	1,577	3,380	863	1,599	18,065	18,420	9,042	10,239
Nonfat dry milk*	Lb.	35,893	23,411	4,269	2,514	89,935	331,453	46,726	34,786
Eggs, in the shell	Doz.	1,052	1,471	978	1,068	23,511	14,985	11,618	7,869
Hides and skins 3/	No.	616	1,015	4,142	7,874	5,630	5,464	33,706	46,091
Beef and veal, total 4/	Lb.	1,470	2,158	700	861	16,633	20,690	6,582	7,943
Pork, total 4/	Lb.	7,500	5,515	1,861	1,606	39,905	49,067	13,828	14,128
Variety meats 5/	Lb.	6,690	11,346	1,589	2,162	57,267	72,291	13,822	14,207
Poultry, canned, fresh or frozen 4/	Lb.	3,686	10,305	1,265	2,530	47,409	99,264	15,272	26,791
Lard	Lb.	56,521	50,260	5,946	4,376	290,714	449,391	36,813	41,236
Tallow, edible and inedible	Lb.	74,911	124,598	6,318	8,387	716,770	1,016,762	60,851	73,029
Cotton, unmfd., e cl linters (running bales)	Bale	211	839	26,076	105,900	2,115	4,177	285,898	505,714
Apples, fresh	Lb.	13,760	27,590	1,024	2,295	85,922	146,419	7,066	12,175
Oranges and tangerines, fresh	Lb.	40,713	41,488	2,569	2,944	240,377	325,958	19,203	23,104
Prunes, dried	Lb.	3,418	7,225	886	1,731	52,393	61,465	11,764	14,535
Raisins and currants	Lb.	2,587	8,486	704	1,187	38,292	64,261	9,464	10,794
Fruits, canned 6/	Lb.	18,438	18,096	2,900	2,781	209,865	250,076	32,162	34,962
Orange juice	Gal.	1,111	1,806	2,258	2,812	7,532	8,463	14,651	14,476
Barley, grain (48 lb.)	Bu.	5,626	9,027	6,852	10,013	82,722	84,069	94,336	88,572
Corn, grain (56 lb.)*	Bu.	16,575	16,797	22,164	22,755	132,324	145,750	172,786	188,491
Grain sorghums (56 lb.)	Bu.	9,191	8,817	10,486	10,168	68,791	72,985	80,848	81,155
Oats, grain (32 lb.)	Bu.	3,198	1,794	2,450	1,561	19,271	31,630	13,418	22,515
Rice, milled, excludes paddy*	Lb.	59,127	211,829	4,431	14,311	846,584	1,226,269	64,582	79,951
Rye, grain (56 lb.)	Bu.	1,161	88	1,371	120	7,759	3,797	9,569	4,781
Wheat, grain (60 lb.)*	Bu.	28,466	40,081	48,743	66,993	229,006	235,492	392,859	400,320
Flour, wholly of U. S. wheat (100 lb.)*	Bag	2,301	3,781	10,169	15,853	22,506	25,674	101,389	106,750
Oil cake and oil-cake meal (2,000 lb.)	Ton	42	58	2,763	3,845	322	707	20,856	46,226
Flaxseed (56 lb.)	Bu.	36	22	127	75	4,914	7,131	14,482	23,047
Soybeans, except canned (60 lb.)	Bu.	8,400	7,698	19,147	17,759	70,296	90,387	162,058	205,448
Soybean oil, crude, refined, etc.	Lb.	10,169	56,416	1,305	5,833	523,862	597,849	67,620	66,221
Cottonseed oil, crude, refined, etc.	Lb.	17,112	78,650	1,961	8,618	100,809	430,741	12,537	55,011
Tobacco, unmanufactured	Lb.	17,019	25,452	11,972	19,423	365,160	361,523	271,890	272,153
Beans, dried*	Lb.	23,352	17,199	1,843	1,503	167,464	288,025	13,323	22,65
Peas, dried (except cowpeas and chickpeas)	Lb.	18,677	12,545	1,229	735	116,556	155,201	7,272	10,092
Potatoes, white	Lb.	11,084	14,133	237	379	190,916	179,503	4,756	4,851
Vegetables, canned 6/	Lb.	8,103	7,126	1,146	1,095	63,433	61,275	9,781	9,308
Other agricultural commodities				36,238	44,104			332,089	389,827
TOTAL AGRICULTURAL COMMODITIES				249,585	399,123			2,501,488	2,984,415
TOTAL NONAGRICULTURAL COMMODITIES				1,016,377	1,160,063			8,943,404	9,00,032
TOTAL ALL COMMODITIES				1,265,962	1,559,186			11,444,892	11,985,447

1/ Preliminary. 2/ At place of export. 3/ Excludes the weight of "other hides and skins", reported in value only. 4/ Product weight. 5/ Includes beef and pork livers, beef tongues, and other variety meats, fresh or frozen. Product weight. 6/ Includes only classes shown separately in Table 2 of the monthly "Foreign Agricultural Trade".
* Includes "Food exported for relief or charity by individuals and private agencies".

Compiled from official records, Bureau of the Census.

IMPORTS (FOR CONSUMPTION): February 1959 and 1960 and July-February 1958-59 and 1959-60 1/

Commodity imported	Unit	February Quantity 1959	February Quantity 1960	February Value 1959	February Value 1960	July-February Quantity 1958-59	July-February Quantity 1959-60	July-February Value 1958-59	July-February Value 1959-60
		Thousands	Thousands	1,000 dollars	1,000 dollars	Thousands	Thousands	1,000 dollars	1,000 dollars
SUPPLEMENTARY									
Cattle, dutiable	No.	69	65	7,567	6,395	776	361	91,511	39,104
Casein or lactarene	Lb.	7,132	6,028	1,340	1,192	60,022	53,368	11,382	10,466
Cheese	Lb.	4,853	4,333	2,174	2,125	39,171	42,241	18,862	21,162
Hides and skins	Lb.	13,527	9,572	5,334	4,448	98,558	96,145	38,067	48,074
Beef and veal, total 2/	Lb.	38,945	33,232	14,935	11,397	345,655	435,488	121,295	151,874
Pork, total 2/	Lb.	12,900	14,246	8,834	9,714	129,168	106,184	85,981	70,554
Mutton, goat and lamb, fresh or frozen 2/	Lb.	2,722	4,105	689	813	20,055	34,619	4,998	7,484
Sausage casings	Lb.	1,090	1,146	848	932	10,193	9,815	8,402	7,125
Wool, unmfd., e cxl free, etc. (actual weight)	Lb.	17,210	13,646	10,626	10,097	86,114	90,708	58,180	63,403
Cotton, unmfd., excl. interi (480 lb.)	Bale	2	6	209	605	125	134	23,742	20,529
Jute and jute butts, unmfd. (2,240 lb.)	Ton	9	10	1,693	1,966	22	47	4,367	7,756
Olives in brine	Gal.	1,001	1,238	1,562	1,522	8,675	8,935	13,055	12,447
Pineapples, canned, prepared or preserved	Lb.	6,210	12,372	689	1,355	51,638	74,163	6,044	8,553
Barley, grain (48 lb.)	Bu.	46	574	63	782	8,299	10,900	990	14,330
Oats, grain (32 b.)	Bu.	134	232	153	297	2,665	1,363	2,226	1,374
Wheat, gra h (60 lb.)	Bu.	956	780	1,449	1,368	4,745	4,502	7,342	7,283
Feeds and fodders	3/	3/	3/	1,402	685	3/	3/	10,726	5,343
Nuts and preparations				4,270	4,501			47,557	47,994
Copra	Lb.	36,214	45,766	3,473	4,208	385,385	464,052	32,667	43,397
Vegetable o sl fats, and wa os, expressed	Lb.	36,618	32,461	7,474	6,656	351,020	331,207	61,201	58,368
Seeds, field and garden	3/	3/	3/	1,011	1,641	3/		8,738	14,187
Sugar, cane (2,000 lb.)	Ton	344	398	37,658	42,398	2,762	2,748	306,593	298,773
Molasses, unf k for human consumption	Gal.	17,295	26,076	2,352	2,350	187,626	164,320	22,666	16,910
Tobacco, unmanufactured	Lb.	11,804	12,753	8,505	9,538	101,749	103,396	75,540	76,043
Tomatoes, natural state	Lb.	50,366	73,449	3,807	5,476	85,553	157,158	6,312	12,384
Other supplementary				24,308	24,652			218,480	204,181
Total supplementary				152,425	157,113			1,236,924	1,269,098
COMPLEMENTARY									
Silk, raw	Lb.	419	376	1,410	1,595	3,470	4,925	11,710	19,308
Wool, unmfd., free in bond (actual weight)	Lb.	17,616	17,292	8,122	9,300	138,092	137,388	62,521	73,181
Bananas	Bunch	4,224	5,260	5,732	6,951	30,898	35,494	43,875	49,351
Cocoa or cacao beans	Lb.	34,400	40,314	12,688	11,570	269,989	294,749	103,568	93,381
Coffee (incl. into Puerto Rico)	Lb.	301,457	284,055	108,200	101,744	1,853,105	2,025,751	744,843	709,802
Coffee essences, substitutes, etc.	Lb.	676	431	1,256	740	3,075	3,033	6,867	5,432
Tea	Lb.	8,635	11,416	4,269	5,424	69,645	74,552	32,774	35,690
Spices (complementary)	Lb.	5,227	11,796	2,008	5,825	55,979	62,323	21,654	24,722
Abaca or Manila (2,240 lb.)	Ton	3	11	1,288	634	30	20	9,828	9,282
Sisal and henequen (2,240 lb.)	Ton	10	11	1,420	1,815	76	79	10,948	13,101
Rubber, crude	Lb.	109,574	91,725	29,525	32,694	787,868	808,448	189,437	267,196
Other complementary				5,529	7,718			46,930	58,272
Total complementary				181,447	186,010			1,284,955	1,358,718
TOTAL AGRICULTURAL COMMODITIES				333,872	343,123			2,581,879	2,627,816
TOTAL NONAGRICULTURAL COMMODITIES				779,424	945,466			6,247,472	7,507,025
TOTAL ALL COMMODITIES				1,113,296	1,288,589			8,829,351	10,134,841

1/ Preliminary. 2/ Product weight. 3/ Reported in value only.

Compiled from official records, Bureau of the Census.

UNITED STATES DEPARTMENT OF AGRICULTURE
WASHINGTON 25, D. C.

Official Business

FOREIGN AGRICULTURAL TRADE

Digest

OF THE UNITED STATES   **MAY 1960**

Issued monthly by Foreign Agricultural Service, United States Department of Agriculture, Washington 25, D.C.   Free within U.S. on request.   Also available are monthly and yearly Foreign Agricultural Trade Statistical Reports, containing detailed statistics on quantity and value of exports and imports.

EXPORT   HIGHLIGHTS

Agricultural exports in July-March 1959-60 moved at near-record pace in value, at record rate in volume. Exports of $3,373 million in July-March 1959-60 were 21 percent larger than the $2,794 million in the corresponding period a year earlier. In volume, exports were over one-fourth larger this year over last and set a new record. Nearly half of the $579 million increase was the result of larger cotton exports. Other substantial gains were in soybeans ($48 million), animals and animal products ($48 million), vegetable oils ($44 million), and wheat ($29 million). Small reductions occurred in dairy products, barley, rye, and grain sorghums. Tobacco exports were close to the level in 1958-59.

U. S. agricultural exports, July-March

Commodity	1958-59	1959-60	Chg.
	Million dollars		Pct.
Cotton	321	605	+88
Grains & feeds 1/	1,134	1,229	+8
Wheat & flour 1/	569	598	+5
Feed grains 1/ 2/	399	416	+4
Rice, milled 1/	74	96	+30
Tobacco, unmfd.	295	292	-1
Veg. oils & seeds	298	404	+36
Soybeans	174	222	+28
Ed. veg. oils 3/	87	131	+51
Fruits & preps.	171	192	+12
Vegs. & preps. 1/	93	109	+17
Animals & prods. 1/	394	442	+12
Fats & oils	117	139	+19
Meats & prods.	70	85	+21
Hides & skins	39	53	+36
Dairy products 1/	109	96	-12
Other 1/	88	100	+33
Total	2,794	3,373	+21

1/ Includes private relief, starting with March 1960 issue. 2/ Excludes products.
3/ Cottonseed and soybean.

March exports were one-third larger this year. March agricultural exports of $388 million in 1960 were $96 million greater than the $292 million in 1959. Cotton accounted for two-thirds of the rise; wheat, 16 percent; vegetable oils and oilseeds, 8 percent; and rice, 7 percent. Exports of animals and animal products, feed grains, vegetables and preparations, and fruits and preparations remained close to 1959 levels. Tobacco exports were somewhat lower this year.

Exports were up to all major areas except Oceania. Agricultural exports moved in larger amount this year to all of the major world areas with the exception of Oceania. July-March 1959-60 exports to Europe totaled $1,652 million, up 25 percent over a year earlier; Asia, $854 million, up 15 percent; Latin America, $403 million, up 4 percent; and Africa, $144 million, up 153 percent. Exports to Oceania (including Australia) of $30 million were 15 percent less. Europe accounted for nearly 60 percent of the overall gain owing primarily to increased shipments of cotton. Individual value gains for major West European countries ranged from a high of $134 million for the United Kingdom, the largest foreign outlet for U. S. agricultural products, to a low of $18 million for Denmark. Outside of Europe, substantial increases were made in exports to Japan, Canada, Egypt, Venezuela, and Brazil. There were declines in exports to India, Cuba, Republic of Korea, and Mexico.

COTTON   March 1960 cotton exports, excluding linters, totaled 767 thousand running bales. This was 483 thousand bales more than in March a year earlier. July-March exports of 4,944 thousand bales in 1959-60 were more than double the 2,399 thousand in 1958-59. The major foreign markets were Western Europe, Japan, and Canada. For the rest of this fiscal year, exports are expected to move at the high level of recent months. For the year, they should total about 6.5 million bales compared with 3.1 million in 1958-59. Principal factors in the expansion of cotton exports were increased consumption in major textile manufacturing countries following the 1958 textile recession, large exportable supplies of U. S. cotton at competitive prices, and smaller exportable supplies in major foreign producing countries.

GRAINS AND FEEDS   Wheat exports in July-March were about 25 million bushels ahead of a year earlier. July-March wheat and flour exports, including USDA welfare donations, were 349 million bushels in 1959-60, 8 percent greater than the 324 million in 1958-59. March exports totaled 54 million bushels this year compared with 52 million in 1959. For the year as a whole, exports are expected to total 475 million bushels, 32 million larger than in 1958-59. This year's gain mainly reflects increased exports under Title I of Public Law 480.

U. S. agricultural exports by country of destination, July-March 1958-59 and 1959-60

Country	1958-59	1959-60	Chg.
	Million dollars		Pct.
United Kingdom	248	382	+54
Japan	242	322	+33
West Germany	208	293	+41
Canada	248	290	+17
Netherlands	182	264	+45
India	191	165	-14
Italy	85	118	+39
Belgium	81	106	+31
Cuba	110	95	-14
France	51	90	+76
Egypt	12	78	+550
Venezuela	66	72	+9
Poland	56	61	+9
Rep. of Korea	67	54	-19
Brazil	34	52	+53
Denmark	34	52	+53
Mexico	58	47	-19
Other	821	832	+1
Total	2,794	3,373	+21

March feed grain exports were slightly less than those of a year earlier. Feed grain exports of 780 thousand short tons in March 1960 were 2 percent below the 797 thousand in 1959. July-March exports of 9.4 million tons were 8 percent greater than the 8.7 million in 1958-59. Corn accounted for 48 percent of feed grain exports; grain sorghums and barley, 23 percent each; and oats, 6 percent. Europe continued to be the major foreign outlet, taking about 70 percent of the total. Exports

- Continued on page 4 -

TRADE NEWS ROUNDUP

On May 4 USDA announced its largest Title I Public Law 480 agreement to date. The new agreement--part of the President's Food-for-Peace Program-- provides for the sale over the next 4 years of $1,276 million worth of wheat and rice to India and is also the first to include substantial amounts for reserves: Of the 587 million bushels of wheat, 147 million will be kept as a reserve; all of the 22 million bags of rice will be used for this purpose. India will use the reserves to combat inflationary pressures caused by shortages and uneven distribution of foodstuffs.

—————————O—————————

A substantial increase in U. S. overseas grain exports through the St. Lawrence Seaway is in sight for 1960. Some ports on the Great Lakes are predicting increases ranging from one-fourth to one-third. Optimism stems from improvements in efficiency resulting from last year's experience with grain shipments; improvements in channel, harbor, and transfer facilities; and reduced levels of overland freight rates to Great Lake ports.

—————————O—————————

Production in excess of effective demand dominates the world wheat situa- tion, reports the Twenty-ninth Session of the International Wheat Council, held in London April 5-12. The major issue concerns the adjustments that are needed to balance supply and effective demand and also the need for both exporters and importers to share responsibility for making these ad- justments. Wheat consumption is static or declining in highly developed areas and increasing in less developed countries. Surplus disposal opera- tions go some way in meeting the great potential demand in less developed countries, but the Council points out that these should be undertaken with minimum interference to commercial exports of third countries.

—————————O—————————

A multilateral tariff conference under the General Agreement on Tariffs and Trade (GATT) is scheduled to begin this September at Geneva, Switzer- land. The conference will provide this country with opportunities to expand foreign markets by reducing tariff barriers abroad. With the pro- gressive removal of import restrictions on U. S. products for balance-of- payments reasons, tariffs have become more significant. Of particular importance to U. S. exports will be negotiations with the European Eco- nomic Community--the Common Market--aimed at keeping its external tariff as low as feasible toward the United States and other outside countries.

—————————O—————————

The Foreign Agricultural Service observes its 30th anniversary on June 5. It began in 1930 as a division in the former Bureau of Agricultural Eco- nomics. During the war and postwar period, it was the Office of Foreign Agricultural Relations. In 1953 the agency reassumed its original name and was strengthened to increase assistance to U. S. agriculture in ex- panding foreign markets. The attaches, who had been transferred to the Department of State in 1939, were returned to USDA in 1953.

to Europe for the remainder of this fiscal year are expected to increase
somewhat, reflecting the need for grains before the European harvest.
Total feed grain exports are expected to be 6 to 8 percent larger than a
year ago.

Rice exports in July-March were up 45 percent this year. Exports of milled
rice totaled 14.4 million bags in July-March 1959-60 compared with 9.9 million in 1958-59. March shipments of 2.2 million bags were 47 percent
larger than 1.5 million in 1959. The improved rice export situation reflected mainly increased shipments under Title I of Public Law 480. Exports to Cuba--the largest foreign outlet for U. S. rice--were about 20
percent below those of a year earlier.

TOBACCO   July-March tobacco exports were slightly below those of a year
          earlier. Unmanufactured tobacco exports of 389 million pounds
(declared export weight) in July-March 1959-60 were 2 percent below the
398 million in July-March 1958-59. Value was down less due to higher
prices for U. S. leaf this season. Exports for the entire fiscal year
are expected to approach the 473 million pounds exported last year.

VEGETABLE OILS   July-March exports of soybeans were 31 percent above a
AND OILSEEDS   year ago. July-March exports of soybeans totaled 98 mil-
                 lion bushels compared with the previous year's 9-month
total of 75 million. Most of the increase was due to larger shipments to
Western Europe, reflecting strong demand for both oil and meal. Exports
for the current fiscal year are likely to reach 125 million bushels, 22
million larger than last year.

Edible vegetable oil exports for dollars were up substantially. July-
March combined shipments of cottonseed oil and soybean oil totaled 1,123
million pounds compared with the previous year's 683 million pounds. The
increase reflected primarily larger shipments for dollars to Western
Europe. July-March exports under Title I of Public Law 480 this fiscal
year were slightly less than in the same period last year. Other major
vegetable oil exporters had smaller exportable supplies this year. Exports
for the current fiscal year probably will be the heaviest on record.

FRUITS AND   Exports of fruits and preparations were larger this July-
PREPARATIONS March. July-March exports of fruits and preparations
              totaled $192 million in 1959-60 compared with the $171 mil-
lion in 1958-59. Increases occurred in fresh apples, fresh oranges, dried
prunes, raisins, and canned fruits. The favorable supply situation in the
United States and prosperous conditions in Western Europe along with some
recent dollar liberalization there were principal factors in larger exports
this year.

VEGETABLES AND   Exports of dried beans and peas were up substantially in
PREPARATIONS   July-March. Larger exports of dried beans and peas
                 accounted for most of the increase in July-March exports
of vegetables and preparations from $93 million in 1958-59 to $109 million
in 1959-60. The heavy exports of dried beans and peas reflected reduced
crops in Europe and Latin America.

ANIMALS AND   Exports of lard and tallow in July-March were substan-
ANIMAL PRODUCTS   tially above the same period a year earlier. July-March
                   exports of lard totaled 505 million pounds in 1959-60,
53 percent more than the 330 million in 1958-59. The United Kingdom is
now the major foreign outlet for lard, taking over half of total exports.
Most of the lard for the United Kingdom was shipped in tankers; bulk han-
dling has reduced prices in foreign markets by about 10 percent. Exports
of tallow totaled 1,158 million pounds in 1959-60, 41 percent above the
820 million in 1958-59. Increased slaughtering of cattle at heavier
weights resulted in larger tallow output available for export at competitive prices. About half of U. S. tallow production is marketed overseas,
principally in Italy, Japan, and the Netherlands.

IMPORT HIGHLIGHTS

July-March agricultural imports were slightly ahead this fiscal year.
July-March imports for consumption amounted to $2,991 million in fiscal
year 1959-60 compared with $2,953 million last year. All of the increase
was accounted for by complementary (noncompetitive) products as supplementary (somewhat competitive) products were below those of a year earlier.

Supplementary imports this July-March were 2 percent less than a year ago.
July-March supplementary imports of $1,447 million in 1959-60 were $29 million below the $1,476 million last year. Principal value declines were in
dutiable cattle and pork. Other value declines occurred in cotton, cane
sugar, grains and feeds, and vegetable oils. There were increases in beef,
hides and skins, and oilbearing materials.

Complementary imports were 5 percent larger this July-March. July-March
complementary imports increased to $1,543 million in 1959-60, $67 million
above the $1,476 million last year. The most significant value increase
in this group was the $81 million gain in rubber. Other value increases
were in silk, carpet wool, bananas, tea, and spices. Value declines occurred in coffee and cocoa beans, but their quantities were larger than a
year earlier.

March import decline reflected mainly lower prices for complementary products. March imports fell to $363 million in 1960 from the $371 million in
1959. Supplementary imports of $178 million were about the same as in 1959.
Imports of dutiable cattle, sugar, and molasses were above those of a year
earlier in value, but declines occurred in pork, wheat, and fresh tomatoes.
Beef imports were only slightly above a year earlier. Complementary imports
of $185 million were somewhat smaller, primarily as the result of value de-
clines in imports of cocoa beans and coffee due to lower prices.

DOMESTIC EXPORTS: March 1959 and 1960 and July-March 1958-59 and 1959-60 1/

Commodity exported	Unit	Quantity March 1959 (Thousands)	Quantity March 1960 (Thousands)	Value 2/ March 1959 (1,000 dollars)	Value 2/ March 1960 (1,000 dollars)	Quantity July-March 1958-59 (Thousands)	Quantity July-March 1959-60 (Thousands)	Value 2/ July-March 1958-59 (1,000 dollars)	Value 2/ July-March 1959-60 (1,000 dollars)
Cheese*	Lb.	1,075	773	430	352	48,933	12,525	3,650	4,908
Evaporated milk*	Lb.	5,311	8,250	743	1,315	87,823	75,856	14,092	11,771
Dried whole milk	Lb.	1,812	3,687	982	1,709	19,677	22,107	10,023	11,948
Nonfat dry milk*	Lb.	51,322	29,047	5,550	2,973	461,258	360,500	52,276	37,759
Eggs, in the shell	Doz.	823	1,514	1,065	1,170	24,335	16,498	12,684	9,039
Hides and skins 3/	No.	760	939	5,019	6,941	6,391	6,402	38,725	53,032
Beef and veal, total 4/	Lb.	1,850	2,201	839	898	18,482	22,891	7,421	8,842
Pork, total 4/	Lb.	4,824	7,828	1,573	1,998	44,729	56,896	15,402	16,127
Variety meats 5/	Lb.	7,287	8,782	1,698	1,693	64,555	81,073	15,520	15,900
Poultry, canned, fresh or frozen 4/	Lb.	7,190	10,587	2,231	2,806	54,599	109,850	17,503	29,597
Lard	Lb.	41,910	55,506	4,589	4,963	332,624	504,897	41,402	46,199
Tallow, edible and inedible	Lb.	103,071	141,011	8,275	9,093	819,841	1,157,773	69,126	82,122
Cotton, unmfd., excl. linters	Bales	284	767	35,599	99,560	2,399	4,944	321,497	605,274
Cotton linters runhing bales	Bales	6,171	11,375	500	878	92,093	157,795	7,567	13,053
Apples, fresh	Lb.	55,787	47,898	3,538	3,539	296,164	373,857	22,740	26,643
Oranges and tangerines, fresh	Lb.	3,798	4,674	980	1,164	56,914	66,138	12,744	15,699
Prunes, dried	Lb.	2,304	6,405	614	881	40,597	70,666	10,078	11,675
Raisins and currants	Lb.	19,222	18,374	3,080	2,065	229,087	268,449	35,242	37,626
Fruits, canned 6/	Lb.	1,334	1,162	2,421	1,867	8,866	9,625	17,072	16,344
Orange juice 6/	Gal.	7,401	8,200	8,359	9,070	90,123	92,708	102,694	97,641
Barley, grain (48 lb.)	Bu.	13,576	14,808	17,964	19,575	45,901	160,558	190,755	208,067
Corn, grain (56 lb.)*	Bu.	7,334	5,007	8,831	5,540	76,126	77,993	89,679	86,695
Grain sorghums (56 lb.)	Bu.	2,094	1,759	1,524	1,540	2,365	33,389	14,943	24,006
Oats, grain (32 lb.)	Bu.	146,269	216,885	8,966	16,122	992,853	1,443,154	73,547	96,073
Rice, milled, excludes paddy*	Lb.	220	80	268	109	7,979	3,877	9,837	4,889
Rye, grain (56 lb.)	Bu.	37,130	43,166	65,344		266,135	278,658		
Wheat, grain (60 lb.)*	Bu.	2,273	4,476	9,724	72,659	24,779	30,149	458,203	472,978
Flour, wholly of U. S. wheat (60 lb.)*	Bag	47	41	3,057	17,815	369	748	111,113	124,565
Oil cake and oil-cake meal (2,000 lb.)	Ton	0	2	0	2,760	4,914	7,133	23,912	48,985
Flaxseed (56 lb.)	Bu.	5,023	7,168	2	8	75,319	97,556	4,488	23,055
Soybeans, except canned (60 lb.)	Bu.	49,361	52,332	11,547	16,506	573,222	650,181	173,605	221,995
Soybean oil, crude, refined, etc.	Lb.	8,893	42,317	5,688	5,605	609,702	473,058	73,307	71,316
Cottonseed oil, crude, refined, etc.	Lb.	33,219	27,754	1,128	4,547	398,379	389,277	13,665	59,558
Tobacco, unmanufactured	Lb.	26,080	12,229	23,451	20,334	193,544	300,255	295,342	292,487
Beans, dried*	Lb.	12,104	15,677	2,108	1,035	128,661	170,878	15,431	23,640
Peas, dried (except cowpeas and chickpeas)	Lb.	10,958	26,269	899	972	201,874	205,772	8,171	11,064
Potatoes, white	Lb.	7,666	9,349	268	765	71,099	70,624	5,024	5,615
Vegetables, canned 9/	Lb.			99	1,421			10,780	10,729
Other agricultural commodities				42,190	45,852			374,380	435,677
TOTAL AGRICULTURAL COMMODITIES				292,046	388,190			2,793,534	3,372,605
TOTAL NONAGRICULTURAL COMMODITIES				1,149,278	1,344,909			10,092,682	10,345,941
TOTAL ALL COMMODITIES				1,441,324	1,733,099			12,886,216	13,718,546

1/ Preliminary. 2/ At place of export. 3/ Excludes the weight of "other hides and skins", reported in value only. 4/ Product weight. 5/ Includes beef and pork livers, beef tongues, and other variety meats, fresh or frozen. Product weight. 6/ Includes only classes shown separately in Table 2 of the monthly "Foreign Agricultural Trade".
* Includes "Food exported for relief or charity by individuals and private agencies".

Compiled from official records, Bureau of the Census.

IMPORTS (FOR CONSUMPTION): March 1959 and 1960 and July-March 1958-59 and 1959-60 1/

Commodity Imported	Unit	March Quantity 1959	March Quantity 1960	March Value 1959	March Value 1960	July-March Quantity 1958-59	July-March Quantity 1959-60	July-March Value 1958-59	July-March Value 1959-60
		Thousands	Thousands	1,000 dollars	1,000 dollars	Thousands	Thousands	1,000 dollars	1,000 dollars
SUPPLEMENTARY									
Cattle, dutiable	No.	64	77	7,399	8,244	840	437	98,910	47,348
Casein or lactarene	lb.	10,934	11,225	2,158	2,205	70,956	64,593	13,540	12,670
Cheese	lb.	5,649	5,245	2,487	2,640	44,819	47,486	21,348	23,802
Hides and skins	lb.	24,183	18,451	9,317	8,548	122,741	114,596	47,384	56,622
Beef and veal, tota 2/	lb.	28,767	32,887	11,051	11,468	374,422	468,376	132,346	163,342
Pork, total 2/	lb.	16,538	11,832	11,241	7,847	145,706	118,016	97,222	78,401
Mutton, goat and lamb, fresh or frozen 2/	lb.	2,314	4,162	66	797	22,369	38,781	5,604	8,281
Sausage casings	lb.	1,287	1,338	843	1,090	11,480	11,153	9,245	8,215
Wool, unmfd., e cxl free, etc. (actual weight)	lb.	18,973	14,340	10,861	10,425	105,087	105,048	69,041	73,827
Cotton, umfd., e cxl linters (480 lb.)	Bale	3	4	335	453	129	139	24,076	20,892
Jute and jute butts, umfd. (2,240 lb.)	Ton	7	11	1,468	1,648	29	58	5,836	9,404
Olives in brine	Gal.	1,400	1,212	2,194	1,484	0,075	10,147	15,249	13,931
Pineapples, canned, prepared or preserved	lb.	7,637	7,768	815	940	59,275	81,931	6,859	9,493
Barley, gra h (48 lb.)	Bu.	1,093	1,159	1,523	1,543	9,391	12,059	12,513	15,873
Oats, grain (32 lb.)	Bu.	175	140	193	173	2,840	1,503	2,419	1,547
Wheat, grain (60 lb.)	Bu.	1,428	747	2,305	1,334	6,173	5,249	9,646	8,617
Feeds and fodders		3/	3/	1,234	838	3/	3/	11,960	6,182
Nuts and preparations				3,880	4,385			51,438	52,379
Copra	lb.	42,896	54,432	4,315	5,217	428,281	518,484	36,982	48,614
Vegetable o s fats, and we s, expressed	lb.	47,842	44,316	8,758	8,258	398,862	375,522	69,959	66,626
Seeds, field and garden		3/		819	1,600	3/		9,556	15,787
Sugar, cane (2,000 lb.)	Ton	438	477	47,611	50,186	3,200	3,225	354,205	348,959
Molasses, unfit for human consumption	Gal.	16,877	40,314	1,703	3,622	204,503	204,634	24,369	20,532
Tobacco, unmanufactured	lb.	12,883	13,115	9,496	9,665	114,632	116,511	85,035	85,708
Tomatoes, natural state	lb.	86,115	76,199	6,358	5,361	171,669	233,356	12,670	17,745
Other supplementary				30,585	28,304			249,067	232,516
Total supplementary				179,555	178,275			1,476,479	1,447,373
COMPLEMENTARY									
Silk, raw	lb.	379	484	1,382	2,073	3,849	5,409	13,092	21,381
Wool, unmfd., free in bond (actual weight)	lb.	28,603	24,449	12,927	13,506	166,695	161,837	75,448	86,687
Bananas	Bunch	5,770	5,100	8,027	7,403	36,668	40,594	51,902	56,754
Cocoa or cacao be ms	lb.	43,012	45,009	14,753	12,359	313,001	339,758	118,320	105,939
Coffee (nc l into Puerto Rico)	lb.	298,053	267,087	105,952	95,146	2,151,158	2,292,838	850,795	804,948
Coffee essences, substitutes, etc.	lb.	502	491	1,008	860	3,576	3,524	7,874	6,292
Tea	lb.	9,057	11,593	4,286	6,108	78,702	86,45	37,060	41,798
Spices (complementary)	lb.	7,565	9,152	3,664	5,523	63,545	71,476	25,318	30,245
Abaca or Manila (2,240 lb.)	Ton	5	1	1,600	536	34	21	1,428	9,918
Sisal and henequen (2,240 lb.)	Ton	2	9	2,680	1,525	88	88	13,627	14,626
Rubber, crude	lb.	108,829	86,421	28,963	31,355	896,697	894,869	218,401	298,551
Other complementary				6,624	7,597			53,226	66,170
Total complementary				191,536	184,591			1,476,491	1,543,309
TOTAL AGRICULTURAL COMMODITIES				371,091	362,866			2,952,970	2,990,682
TOTAL NONAGRICULTURAL COMMODITIES				902,875	1,003,235			7,150,347	8,510,260
TOTAL ALL COMMODITIES				1,273,966	1,366,101			10,103,317	11,500,942

1/ Preliminary. 2/ Product weight. 3/ Reported in value only.

Compiled from official records, Bureau of the Census.

UNITED STATES DEPARTMENT OF AGRICULTURE
WASHINGTON 25, D. C.

Official Business

FOREIGN AGRICULTURAL TRADE Digest

OF THE UNITED STATES

JUNE 1960

Issued monthly by Foreign Agricultural Service, United States Department of Agriculture, Washington 25, D.C. Free within U.S. on request. Also available are monthly and yearly Foreign Agricultural Trade Statistical Reports, containing detailed statistics on quantity and value of exports and imports.

EXPORT HIGHLIGHTS

July-April agricultural exports in 1959-60 were up 22 percent. Agricultural exports of $3,770 million were $680 million larger than the $3,090 million in 1958-59. Exports moved at an annual rate of $4.5 billion, second highest on record. Volume--nearly 30 percent larger than a year earlier--set a new record.

About half of the value rise took place in cotton. Cotton exports gained $339 million. Other commodities which showed substantial value increases were wheat and flour, $69 million; animals and animal products, $53 million; soybeans, $45 million; edible vegetable oils, $41 million; fruits and vegetables, $36 million; and rice, $31 million. Exports of tobacco, dairy products, and rye ran slightly below the levels in 1958-59.

April 1960 exports totaled almost $100 million more than a year earlier. Agricultural exports of $393 million in April 1960 were one-third larger than those of $296 million in April 1959. Over one-half of the increase was accounted for by cotton shipments, and the remainder mainly by gains in wheat and rice. Wheat exports in April reached a record high, and rice exports more than doubled those in 1959. Exports of vegetable oils and oilseeds, vegetables and preparations, and tobacco were somewhat less while those of animals and animal products, feed grains, and fruits and preparations were about the same as a year earlier.

U. S. agricultural exports, July-April

Commodity	1958-59	1959-60	Chg.
	Million dollars		Pct.
Cotton	353	692	+96
Grains & feeds 1/	1,253	1,404	+12
Wheat & flour 1/	635	704	+11
Feed grains 1/ 2/	435	459	+6
Rice, milled 1/	81	112	+38
Tobacco, unmfd.	313	302	-4
Veg. oils & seeds	343	442	+29
Soybeans	196	241	+23
Ed. veg. oils 3/	106	147	+39
Fruits & preps.	188	211	+12
Vegs. & preps. 1/	106	119	+12
Animals & prods. 1/	439	492	+12
Fats & oils	131	156	+19
Meats & prods.	77	96	+25
Hides & skins	43	58	+35
Dairy products 1/	120	104	-13
Other 1/	95	108	+14
Total	3,090	3,770	+22

1/ Includes private relief, starting with January 1960 data in the March 1960 issue. 2/ Excludes products. 3/ Cottonseed and soybean.

COTTON   Cotton exports this July-April were 3 million bales larger than a year earlier. July-April cotton exports, excluding linters, increased to 5.6 million running bales in fiscal year 1959-60 from the 2.6 million in the previous year. April exports of 669 thousand bales were 173 percent above the level a year earlier. Registrations under the payment-in-kind export program were 6.8 million bales as of June 17. For the fiscal year as a whole, exports are now expected to reach 6.7 million bales in 1959-60 compared with 3.1 million in 1958-59. The substantial gain is due to relatively low export prices for U. S. cotton, a drop in cotton production abroad, record high consumption in foreign free world countries, and some inventory buildup in foreign free world countries.

GRAINS AND FEEDS   Wheat and flour exports are now expected to reach 510 million bushels in fiscal year 1959-60. This estimate is 67 million bushels more than actual exports of 443 million in 1958-59. July-April exports, including USDA donations, were 413 million bushels, 14 percent more than the 362 million in 1958-59. April exports were 64 million bushels, a new record, surpassing the previous peak in April 1951 by 5 million bushels. The increase stemmed from the stepped-up shipments under Title I of Public Law 480. Exports under Title I are expected to total at least 300 million bushels for the year as against 230 million bushels for 1958-59.

Exports of feed grains held up despite increased competition from other major producers in the Western European market. Exports of feed grains in July-April of 1959-60 totaled 10.4 million short tons compared with 9.5 million a year earlier. April exports of 888 thousand short tons in 1960 were about 100 thousand larger than in 1959. Europe has taken over two-thirds of U. S. feed grain exports this fiscal year; more U. S. feed grains were imported to supplement reduced forage production following last summer's drought and to meet increased feed requirements of an expanding livestock industry. Exports have continued to do well this year despite increased competition from other major suppliers, especially Mexico and Argentina, and accumulated stocks of coarse grains on the European Continent. Exports for the remaining months of 1959-60 probably will total about the same as in 1958-59. With the big surge in exports in the first half of fiscal year 1959-60, exports for the full year will be 6 to 8 percent larger than in 1958-59.

April 1960 milled rice exports totaled 2.1 million bags. This was 1.2 million more than in April 1959. July-April exports of 16.6 million bags were 52 percent greater than the 10.9 million in 1958-59. The principal foreign outlets were Western Europe, Indonesia, Cuba, India, and Egypt. The year's total is likely to range between 19 and 20 million bags in fiscal year 1959-60 compared with 14.2 million in 1958-59. About one-half of the exports in 1959-60 is moving under Title I of Public Law 480, which has been the major factor accounting for the improvement.

VEGETABLE OILS   Exports of soybeans remained at record rate. July-April
AND OILSEEDS   soybean exports of 106 million bushels were 25 percent larger than the 85 million shipped in 1958-59. The heavy movement was encouraged by (1) a strong demand for high protein oilseed cakes and meals last summer and fall, (2) availability of large U. S. supplies at competitive prices, and (3) reduced supplies from other major areas, such as peanuts from Africa. The record soybean movement from the

TRADE NEWS ROUNDUP

U. S. agricultural exports in the year ending June 30, 1960, are expected to equal the production from 57 million acres of cropland. This is one acre out of every 6 harvested. Food grains will account for 40 percent of the total export acreage harvested. Feed grains, including those fed to livestock, will account for 22 percent; soybeans, 14 percent; and cotton, 12 percent.

————————O————————

Title I, P.L. 480 agreements announced since mid-May: ...Pakistan: $520 thousand for nonfat dry milk (supplemental agreement). ...Chile: $3.1 million for cotton and tobacco. ...Yugoslavia: $18.8 million for cotton, soybean or cottonseed oil, lemons and lemon juice, and nonfat dry milk.

————————O————————

Agricultural exporters can now get political risk guarantees from U. S. commercial banks and export credit insurance companies under a new program inaugurated by the Export-Import Bank. Guarantees apply to short term transactions and cover risks such as inconvertibility or nontransferability of foreign currencies; imposition of law or regulation which prevents delivery; cancellation of import license; war, hostilities, rebellion, and civil commotion; and expropriation of goods by foreign authorities.

————————O————————

British purchases of U. S. frozen beef and lamb variety meats have been brisk since liberalization of this trade last November. British imports from the United States totaled 5.8 million pounds in the first quarter of 1960 compared with 1.8 million in the like quarter of 1959 and 1.3 million in the same period of 1958.

————————O————————

Japan's record foreign exchange budget for April-September 1960 calls for larger purchases of cotton, wheat, and soybeans than in the October-March period. Under the new budget, Japan's expressed policy for liberalization of trade is taking shape; the Government has earmarked $970 million, or 40 percent of total commodity import funds, for "automatic-approval" licensing. This amount is $270 million greater than in the preceding 6 months, when about 33 percent was set aside.

————————O————————

The U. S. Tariff Commission is investigating the list of import articles which the United States is considering for possible tariff concessions later this year. Concessions--yet to be determined--will be offered to other countries in return for more favorable treatment of U. S. exports in bargaining to take place at a multilateral tariff conference under the General Agreement on Tariffs and Trade. The Commission will determine the articles' "peril points", or limits beyond which concessions might seriously injure domestic industries producing like or directly competitive commodities.

————————O————————

United States has occurred despite recent heavy northbound shipments of soybeans through the Suez Canal, primarily from mainland China. Imports of these beans by Western Europe, particularly West Germany, the United Kingdom, and the Netherlands, increased sharply.

Exports of edible vegetable oils are also expected to set a new record. July-April exports of vegetable oils (cottonseed and soybean) increased to 1,282 million pounds in 1959-60 from the 836 million in 1958-59. All of the gain was in sales for dollars as exports under Government programs were slightly below those of a year earlier. With the prospect of increased exports under Title I of Public Law 480 toward the close of 1959-60 along with the high level of dollar sales throughout the year, exports of vegetable oils in fiscal 1959-60 will surpass the fiscal year 1956-57 record of 1,391 million pounds.

FRUITS AND PREPARATIONS   Exports of major fruit items were larger. July-April exports of fruits and preparations totaled $211 million in 1959-60 compared with $188 million in 1958-59. There were increases in major fruit items like fresh apples, fresh oranges, dried prunes, raisins, and canned fruits. Principal factors in the rise were the large U. S. production, increasingly higher standards of living in industrialized countries, especially in Western Europe, and some recent trade liberalizations.

VEGETABLES AND PREPARATIONS   Smaller exportable supplies after January 1960 limited exports of dry edible beans. July-April exports of vegetables and preparations totaled $119 million in 1959-60 compared with $106 million in 1958-59. The major items are fresh and canned vegetables and dried beans and peas. Vegetable exports in 1959-60 ran about 18 percent larger than in 1958-59 until April when they were only 12 percent larger, reflecting a substantial drop in dried beans. Bean exports stayed well ahead of a year earlier through January 1960, but thereafter they declined sharply due to the smaller U. S. exportable supplies of colored beans.

ANIMALS AND ANIMAL PRODUCTS   Exports of major animal products, except dairy products, were up. July-April exports of animals and animal products of $492 million in 1959-60, including USDA donations, were 12 percent above the $439 million in 1958-59. With the exception of dairy products, all major items—lard, tallow, poultry meats, hides and skins, and meats—were above the same period of 1958-59. Prosperous conditions, along with some trade liberalization in Western Europe and ample U. S. supplies at competitive prices, were the principal factors accounting for the increase. Although total exports of dairy products were somewhat below the level in 1958-59, exports other than USDA donations were up by 22 percent.

Exports of hides and skins were up slightly in volume and substantially in value. Hides and skins exports of 7.2 million pieces in July-April 1959-60 were 3 percent above the 7 million in the same period of 1958-59. Higher cattle hide and calf skin prices caused the export value to increase by 36 percent, which was considerably above the gain in volume. Sharp price increases reflected mainly lower production in the United States, smaller foreign exportable supplies, and the continued strong demand in the industrialized countries.

IMPORT HIGHLIGHTS

Agricultural imports were up slightly. July-April imports totaled $3,329 million, approximately 1 percent ahead of the $3,307 million recorded during the corresponding period of 1958-59. Nominal increases in complementary (noncompetitive) products continued to offset the downward trend in supplementary (competitive) products that has been witnessed throughout the year.

July-April supplementary imports were down 2 percent. July-April supplementary imports totaled $1,626 million, $38 million or 2 percent below 1958-59. Though there were some increases in meat products, apparel wool, vegetables, and fruit products, they were more than offset by declines in dutiable cattle, grains and feeds, vegetable oils and oilseeds, and less significant commodities.

U. S. agricultural imports by country of origin, July-March

Country	1958-59			1959-60		
	Supple-mentary 1/	Comple-mentary 2/	Total	Supple-mentary 1/	Comple-mentary 2/	Total
	- Million dollars -			- Million dollars -		
Brazil	38	360	398	35	360	395
Cuba	287	2	289	282	2	284
Colombia	3/	231	231	3/	215	215
Philippines	152	8	160	173	7	180
Canada	186	2	188	139	2	141
Mexico	108	64	172	83	49	132
Indonesia	1	71	72	1	99	100
Australia	41	3/	41	95	3/	95
New Zealand	72	18	90	66	21	87
Federation of Malaya . . .	3/	51	51	3/	91	91
Argentina	64	27	91	39	28	67
Netherlands	55	11	66	50	14	64
India	25	20	45	31	28	59
Thailand	4	42	46	5	49	54
Belgian Congo	7	28	35	9	42	51
Turkey	42	1	43	45	4	49
Guatemala	3/	45	45	3/	49	49
Ecuador	1	42	43	3/	45	45
Italy	41	3	44	40	4	44
Other	352	450	802	354	434	788
Total	1,476	1,476	2,952	1,447	1,543	2,990

1/ Supplementary imports are somewhat similar to or interchangeable with domestic products. 2/ Complementary imports are generally not competitive with domestic products. 3/ Less than $500 thousand.

IMPORTS (FOR CONSUMPTION): April 1959 and 1960 and July-April 1958-59 and 1959-60 1/

Commodity Imported	Unit	April Quantity 1959 (Thousands)	April Quantity 1960 (Thousands)	April Value 1959 (1,000 dollars)	April Value 1960 (1,000 dollars)	July-April Quantity 1958-59 (Thousands)	July-April Quantity 1959-60 (Thousands)	July-April Value 1958-59 (1,000 dollars)	July-April Value 1959-60 (1,000 dollars)
SUPPLEMENTARY									
Cattle, dutiable	No.	60	79	7,487	6,871	90	517	106,397	54,219
Casein or lactarene	Lb.	8,99	8,137	1,549	1,534	79,455	72,729	15,089	14,204
Cheese	Lb.	4,879	4,738	2,233	2,210	49,69	52,224	23,581	26,012
Hides and skins	Lb.	20,414	13,991	8,594	7,336	143,155	128,587	55,978	63,958
Beef and veal, total 2/	Lb.	52,579	45,933	19,674	16,144	427,001	514,309	152,020	179,486
Pork, total 2/	Lb.	18,829	15,448	11,524	10,728	164,535	133,464	108,746	89,128
Mutton, goat and lamb, fresh or frozen 2/	Lb.	10,144	6,419	2,552	1,363	32,513	45,201	8,156	9,644
Sausage casings	Lb.	1,155	1,187	842	901	12,636	12,340	10,087	9,116
Wool, unmfd., excl. free, etc. (actual weight)	Lb.	15,561	10,282	9,491	8,167	120,648	115,320	78,532	81,90
Cotton, unmfd., excl. linters (480 lb.)	Bale	3	3	231	323	131	142	24,307	21,304
Jute and jute butts, unmfd. (2,240 lb.)	Ton	6	6	1,222	919	35	64	7,057	10,323
Olives in br nb	Lb.	841	1,436	1,291	1,722	10,916	11,583	16,540	15,653
Pineapples, canned, prepared or preserved	Lb.	6,376	9,002	717	1,036	65,651	90,933	7,576	10,529
Barley, grain (48 lb.)	Bu.	305	71	400	105	9,86	12,514	12,913	16,376
Oats, grain (32 lb.)	Bu.	181	131	206	168	3,021	1,634	2,625	1,715
Wheat, grain (60 lb.)	Bu.	744	775	1,052	1,265	6,916	6,025	10,698	9,882
Feeds and fodders				1,277	697			13,237	6,879
Nuts and preparations		3/	3/	3,051	4,812	3/	3/	55,288	57,191
Copra	Lb.	76,622	66,107	7,873	6,395	504,903	584,591	44,855	55,008
Vegetable oils, fats, and waxes, expressed	Lb.	46,228	52,449	8,316	9,604	445,090	427,972	78,276	76,230
Seeds, field and garden		3/	3/	90	1,298	3/		10,506	17,086
Sugar, cane (2,000 b.)	Ton	439	461	46,633	48,251	3,638	3,689	400,837	397,886
Molasses, unfit for human consumption	Gal.	51,242	62,995	5,519	4,654	255,745	269,425	29,888	25,384
Tobacco, unmanufactured	Lb.	11,429	12,734	8,415	9,169	126,062	129,245	93,450	94,877
Tomatoes, natural state	Lb.	56,872	48,751	4,196	3,588	228,540	282,108	16,865	21,333
Other supplementary				31,337	29,201			280,406	260,798
Total supplementary				187,432	177,461			1,663,910	1,626,211
COMPLEMENTARY									
Silk, raw	Lb.	202	50	716	2,232	4,051	5,969	13,808	23,613
Wool, unmfd., free in bond (actual weight)	Lb.	26,251	15,759	12,392	8,990	192,946	177,605	87,840	95,681
Bananas	Bunch	4,607	5,314	7,104	7,793	41,275	45,908	59,006	64,547
Cocoa or oo beans	Lb.	45,281	51,053	15,551	13,492	358,282	390,756	133,871	119,413
Coffee (incl. into Puerto Rico)	Lb.	235,761	217,193	84,304	74,711	2,386,919	2,510,961	935,099	880,173
Coffee essences, substitutes, etc.	Lb.	315	353	545	566	3,891	3,877	8,420	6,857
Tea	Lb.	10,949	9,536	5,074	4,597	89,651	95,681	42,134	46,395
Spices (complementary)	Lb.	8,670	9,780	3,797	6,446	72,215	81,255	29,115	36,690
Abaca or Mani la (2,240 lb.)	Ton	3	4	1,148	2,033	38	25	12,576	11,959
S sal and henequen (2,240 lb.)	Ton	13	6	1,636	1,082	101	94	15,463	15,708
Rubber, crude	Lb.	99,338	81,409	26,242	30,350	996,035	976,278	244,643	328,901
Other complementary				7,492	6,374			60,718	72,639
Total complementary				166,201	158,666			1,642,693	1,702,576
TOTAL AGRICULTURAL COMMODITIES				353,633	336,127			3,306,603	3,328,787
TOTAL NONAGRICULTURAL COMMODITIES				855,400	910,160			8,005,747	9,418,443
TOTAL ALL COMMODITIES				1,209,033	1,246,287			11,312,350	12,747,230

1/ Preliminary.   2/ Product weight.   3/ Reported in value only.

Compiled from official records, Bureau of the Census.

DOMESTIC EXPORTS: April 1959 and 1960 and July-April 1958-59 and 1959-60 1/

Commodity exported	Unit	Quantity (April) 1959	Quantity (April) 1960	Value 2/ (April) 1959	Value 2/ (April) 1960	Quantity (July-April) 1958-59	Quantity (July-April) 1959-60	Value 2/ (July-April) 1958-59	Value 2/ (July-April) 1959-60
		Thousands	Thousands	1,000 dollars	1,000 dollars	Thousands	Thousands	1,000 dollars	1,000 dollars
Cheese*	Lb.	541	707	225	329	49,474	13,232	13,875	5,237
Evaporated milk*	Lb.	4,376	5,623	624	869	92,199	81,479	4,711	12,640
Dried whole milk	Lb.	1,779	4,446	978	2,097	2,656	26,472	11,002	14,003
Nonfat dry milk*	Lb.	65,052	14,531	6,828	1,545	526,310	375,031	59,103	39,304
Eggs, in the shell	Doz.	1,467	1,688	1,146	1,250	25,802	18,187	13,830	10,289
Hides and skins 3/	No.	569	754	3,947	4,997	6,60	7,157	42,671	58,030
Beef and veal, total 4/	Lb.	2,039	2,640	832	1,049	20,521	25,530	8,253	9,891
Pork, total 4/	Lb.	4,431	7,078	1,565	1,945	49,160	63,974	16,967	18,071
Variety meats 5/	Lb.	6,668	7,092	1,565	1,414	71,223	88,165	17,085	7,314
Poultry, canned, fresh or frozen 4/	Lb.	6,479	17,930	1,934	4,986	61,078	127,781	19,437	34,583
Lard	Lb.	41,248	56,154	4,377	5,061	373,873	561,051	45,780	51,261
Tallow, edib & and inedible	Lb.	97,086	160,369	7,818	10,528	916,927	1,318,142	76,944	92,650
Cotton, unmfd, excl. linters (running bales)	Bales	245	669		86,659	2,645	5,611	352,828	691,704
Apples, fresh	Lb.	7,679	9,230	628	634	99,771	167,025	8,95	13,687
Oranges and tangerines, fresh	Lb.	69,205	47,681	4,517	3,401	365,369	421,538	27,258	30,044
Prunes, dried	Lb.	2,932	3,556	768	893	59,123	69,694	3,5 12	16,592
Raisins and currants	Lb.	1,344	5,508	402	833	41,940	76,174	10,480	12,508
Fruits, canned 6/	Lb.	15,268	23,496	2,565	3,498	244,355	291,945	37,807	41,124
Orange juice	Gal.	1,084	1,704	2,026	2,804	9,950	1,329	19,098	19,148
Barley, grain (48 lb.)	Bu.	6,492	5,662	7,448	6,566	96,615	98,362	110,143	104,028
Corn, grain (56 lb.)*	Bu.	16,448	7,752	22,044	23,250	162,349	178,827	212,800	231,956
Grain sorghums (56 lb.)	Bu.	4,839	7,354	5,651	8,360	80,965	85,735	95,331	95,462
Oats, grain (32 lb.)	Bu.	2,071	3,102	1,692	2,718	23,435	38,005	16,635	27,824
Rice, milled, excludes paddy*	Lb.	92,956	212,487	7,163	16,107	1,085,809	1,655,641	80,710	2,180
Rye, grain (56 lb.)	Bu.	65	100	91	140	8,044	3,977	9,929	5,029
Wheat, grain (60 lb.)*	Bu.	31,653	54,949	55,206	91,238	297,788	333,740	513,410	564,949
Flour, wholly of U. S. wheat (100 lb.)*	Bag	2,823	3,814	10,999	14,980	27,603	33,964	122,112	139,545
Oil cake and oil-cake meal (2,000 lb.)*	Ton	45	33	2,962	2,350	414	782	26,874	51,389
Flaxseed (56 lb.)	Bu.	7/	1	2	4	4,915	7,631	4,481	24,597
Soybeans, except canned (60 lb.)	Bu.	9,410	8,471	2,916	19,135	84,729	106,027	195,521	241,089
Soybean oil, crude, refined, etc.	Lb.	57,402	99,975	7,043	9,522	630,625	758,805	850	81,945
Cottonseed oil, crude, refined, etc.	Lb.	96,890	49,876	2,242	5,198	206,592	522,934	25,907	64,756
Tobacco, unmanufactured	Lb.	24,180	14,360	17,414	9,467	422,559	403,636	312,756	301,954
Beans, dried*	Lb.	46,211	8,432	3,804	847	239,755	308,687	19,235	24,487
Peas, dried (except cowpeas and chickpeas)	Lb.	8,455	15,372	702	920	137,116	186,250	8,873	11,984
Potatoes, white	Lb.	22,542	43,823	540	1,532	224,416	249,596	5,564	7,147
Vegetables, canned 6/	Lb.	7,766	4,914	1,095		78,865	75,538	11,875	11,489
Other agricultural commodities				44,212	45,441			418,488	479,049
TOTAL AGRICULTURAL COMMODITIES				296,303	393,327			3,089,838	3,769,839
TOTAL NONAGRICULTURAL COMMODITIES				1,155,831	1,412,534			11,248,513	11,754,569
TOTAL ALL COMMODITIES				1,452,134	1,805,861			14,338,351	15,524,408

1/ Preliminary. 2/ At place of export. 3/ Excludes the weight of "other hides and skins" reported in value only. 4/ Product weight. 5/ Includes beef and pork livers, beef tongues, and other variety meats, fresh or frozen. Product weight. 6/ Includes only classes shown separately in Table 2 of the monthly "Foreign Agricultural Trade". 7/ Less than 500.
* Includes "Food exported for relief or charity by individuals and private agencies".

Compiled from official records, Bureau of the Census.

July-April complementary imports were 4 percent ahead of a year earlier.
July-April complementary (noncompetitive) imports reached a total of $1,703
million, $60 million more than in 1958-59. Principal gains were in rubber,
silk, carpet wool, spices, and tea, with corresponding declines in coffee
and cocoa beans.

April imports totaled less than a year earlier. Both supplementary and complementary imports declined during the month of April as compared with a year
earlier. April 1960 imports equaled $336 million, $18 million below those in
April 1959. Supplementary imports at $177 million were $10 million below
those of a year earlier. Increases in imports of fruits, nuts, vegetable oils
and oilseeds, sugar, and tobacco were more than offset by declines in dutiable
cattle, hides and skins, meat products, and apparel wool. April complementary
imports totaled $159 million, $6 million less than a year earlier. Imports of
coffee, cocoa beans, tea, and carpet wool declined, more than offsetting increases in rubber, silk, and spices.

Most agricultural imports came from a few countries. Although many countries
are involved in the agricultural import trade of the United States, the bulk
of the import trade is concentrated in shipments from a relatively few countries. In July-March of 1959-60, 15 countries accounted for about two-thirds
of U. S. agricultural imports, with values ranging from a high of $395 million
for Brazil to $51 million for Belgian Congo. Another significant point is the
small degree of fluctuation in the value of imports from the major supplying
countries. The major change this year was the $54 million increase in imports
from Australia, reflecting larger shipments of boneless meats. Other increases were noted for the Federation of Malaya, Belgian Congo, Indonesia,
India, Thailand, and the Philippines. Most of these gains were in crude natural rubber and oilbearing materials. Imports from Canada and Mexico declined
primarily because of reduced shipments of dutiable cattle.

FOREIGN AGRICULTURAL TRADE

OF THE UNITED STATES

Digest

JULY - AUGUST 1960

Issued monthly by Foreign Agricultural Service, United States Department of Agriculture, Washington 25, D.C. Free within U.S. on request. Also available are monthly and yearly Foreign Agricultural Trade Statistical Reports, containing detailed statistics on quantity and value of exports and imports.

EXPORT HIGHLIGHTS

Volume of U. S. agricultural exports reached an alltime high in 1959-60. When valued in constant dollars (1952-54 average prices) export volume in the past fiscal year is estimated to have been about 30 percent above the 1958-59 level and 3 percent above the volume in 1956-57, which was the previous record. Increased exports of several major commodities for dollars played a big part in the new record. At the same time, exports under specified Government-financed programs increased slightly.

U. S. agricultural exports, fiscal year

Commodity	1958-59 1/	1959-60 2/	Chg.
	Million dollars		Pct.
Cotton	413	823	+99
Grains & feeds 3/	1,523	1,703	+12
Wheat & flour 3/	776	876	+13
Feed grains 3/ 4/	527	533	+1
Rice, milled 3/	104	137	+32
Tobacco, unmfd.	350	339	-3
Veg. oils & seeds	425	544	+28
Soybeans	238	306	+29
Ed. veg. oils 5/	136	176	+29
Fruits & preps.	229	246	+7
Vegs. & preps. 3/	135	146	+8
Animals & prods. 3/	533	582	+9
Fats & oils	159	186	+17
Meats & prods.	94	114	+21
Hides & skins	55	71	+29
Dairy products 3/	144	121	-16
Other 3/	111	132	+19
Total	3,719	4,515	+21

1/ Partly revised. 2/ Partly estimated. 3/ Includes private relief. 4/ Excludes products. 5/ Cottonseed and soybean.

Value of exports in 1959-60 was second highest on record. Agricultural exports valued at current prices are estimated at $4,515 million, only $213 million under the record $4,728 million in 1956-57, when exports rose substantially due to the Suez crisis and the economic boom in Western Europe. Last year's value was over one-fifth larger than the $3,719 million in fiscal year 1958-59. Cotton accounted for 52 percent of last year's $796 million increase; wheat and flour, 13 percent; soybeans, 9 percent; animals and animal products, 6 percent; cottonseed oil and soybean oil, 5 percent; milled rice, 4 percent; fruits, vegetables, and preparations, 4 percent; and other commodities, 7 percent.

Important export records were set for certain commodities. Export records were set in 1959-60 for feed grains, soybeans, protein meal, poultry meat, tallow, and combined shipments of cottonseed oil and soybean oil. Both wheat and rice exports were the second largest in history, and lard exports were the second largest since World War II. Cotton exports were second highest in over a quarter of a century.

About 71 percent of the year's exports represented dollar sales. Export sales for dollars in fiscal 1959-60 amounted to $3.2 billion--$800 million higher than the previous year's $2.4 billion and second largest in history. This gain reflects to a considerable extent export payments, under payment-in-kind programs, on cotton, wheat, rice, and--part of the time--feed grains. However, shipments of several other commodities for which no payments were made also expanded. These included soybeans, vegetable oils, fruits and fruit juices, and animals and animal products. Only 29 percent of total agricultural exports were under special programs, mainly Public Law 480. Exports under these programs increased by $43 million.

COTTON   Cotton exports in fiscal year 1959-60 are estimated at 6.6 million bales. This was more than twice as much as the 3.1 million running bales in the previous year and was exceeded only once in the past 26 years--in 1956-57. Principal factors in last year's increase were the rising consumption in major textile manufacturing countries following the 1958 textile recession, ample supplies of U. S. cotton at competitive prices, smaller exportable supplies in major foreign producing countries, and some inventory rebuilding in major textile manufacturing countries. Main foreign outlets for U. S. cotton were Western Europe, Japan, and Canada.

GRAINS AND Wheat and flour exports were the second highest in history.
FEEDS   Shipments, estimated at 511 million bushels, were 68 million bushels greater than the 443 million in 1958-59 although 39 million less than the alltime high of 550 million in 1956-57. Exports were equivalent to about one-half of the 1959 crop. The expansion reflected stepped-up shipments under Title I of Public Law 480, which rose from 231 million bushels in 1958-59 to 301 million in 1959-60. Last year's export rise was primarily in increased shipments to UAR-Egypt, Brazil, Poland, Pakistan, Turkey, and Uruguay. India remained the largest foreign outlet, taking over 100 million bushels.

Last year's exports of feed grains topped previous record. Feed grain exports totaled nearly 12 million short tons in 1959-60, exceeding the previous peak in 1958-59 by half a million tons. Exports rose sharply in the first half of 1959-60, but declined in the latter half because of increased competition from other major suppliers, especially Mexico and Argentina. Last year, Western Europe was the largest foreign outlet, taking over two-thirds of U. S. exports. Europe imported more U. S. feed grains to supplement reduced forage production following last summer's drought and to meet increased feed requirements of the expanding livestock industry.

Rice exports were second largest in history. Rice shipments are estimated at 20.5 million bags (100 lbs. each) in fiscal year 1959-60, 44 percent larger than the 14.2 million in 1958-59 and 23 percent below the 26.5 million record in 1956-57. Western Europe, Indonesia, Cuba, India, and Egypt

- Continued on page 4 -

TRADE NEWS ROUNDUP

Five groups of agricultural industry representatives met recently with USDA officials in Washington, D. C. to discuss the U. S. position and actions at the forthcoming negotiations under the General Agreement on Tariffs and Trade (GATT). The discussants called for a lowering of foreign trade barriers hindering exports and voiced concern over new barriers that might arise if draft agricultural policies of the European Economic Community (Common Market) go into effect. Industry groups included those dealing in livestock and livestock products; fats and oils; grains, rice, beans, and peas; poultry; and dairy products.

————————O————————

The Export-Import Bank is lending Japan $40 million to finance purchases of U. S. cotton in the 1960-61 crop year. The new loan--the 12th for cotton since 1948--is $10 million larger than last year's.

————————O————————

The U. S. Tariff Commission has begun a general investigation of competition between California- and foreign-produced fresh fruits and vegetables. The investigation is being undertaken under Section 332 of the Tariff Act of 1930 pursuant to a resolution adopted by the Committee on Ways and Means of the House of Representatives.

————————O————————

Italy on June 15 liberalized dollar imports of fresh, chilled, or frozen red meat (including variety meats); vegetables; oats; oilseeds; sausage; cocoa; sweetened forage; potato flour and flakes; and various starches. However, Italy continues to require licenses for dollar imports of corn, barley, grain sorghums, canned and frozen fruits, fruit and vegetable juices, vegetable oils, poultry products, lard, and honey.

————————O————————

West Germany on July 1 liberalized certain forage and pasture seed imports--6 months sooner than scheduled under GATT.

————————O————————

Title I Public Law 480 agreements announced since mid-June: ...Spain: $64 million for cottonseed and/or soybean oil, cotton, tobacco, barley, and corn. ...Viet-Nam: $800 thousand for wheat and/or wheat flour (supplemental agreement). ...Israel: $7.4 million for feed grains (supplemental agreement). ...Poland: $130 million for wheat, barley, corn, grain sorghums, cotton, cottonseed and/or soybean oil, tobacco, and nonfat dry milk. ...Iran: $3.7 million for wheat.

————————O————————

The recently organized United States Feed Grains Council is expected to give a vigorous new push to exports of feed grains. The Council will work closely with FAS and its export promotion operations, making use of local currencies accruing from Title I Public Law 480 sales.

- Continued from page 2 -

were the principal foreign markets last year. Rice exports to Cuba were about one-fourth less than in 1958-59. About half of all the rice exported from the United States moved under Title I of Public Law 480, which was the main factor in attaining last year's high level.

VEGETABLE OILS AND OILSEEDS   Exports of soybeans set new record. Soybean exports are estimated at 134 million bushels in fiscal year 1959-60, 30 percent larger than the previous record of 103 million in 1958-59. The increase reflected strong foreign demand for high protein oilseed cakes and meals last summer and fall, large exportable supplies of U. S. soybeans at competitive prices, and reduced foreign supplies of other oilseeds and oils. Important foreign outlets were Japan, West Germany, the United Kingdom, and the Netherlands.

Exports of edible vegetable oils surpassed the previous record by 177 million pounds. Exports of vegetable oils (cottonseed and soybean) totaled an estimated 1,570 million pounds in fiscal year 1959-60 compared with 1,079 million a year earlier. Last year's volume was 13 percent larger than the previous record of 1,393 million pounds in 1956-57. The increase over 1958-59 was mainly in dollar sales while exports under Government programs were about the same in both years.

TOBACCO   Exports of tobacco were down by 4 percent in fiscal year 1959-60. Unmanufactured tobacco exports estimated at 455 million pounds were 18 million pounds below the 473 million a year earlier. Developments contributing to the decline were the continuation of foreign trade barriers against U. S. leaf by many of the major importing countries, the relatively higher price for U. S. leaf compared with prices for similar foreign growths, and the record 1960 tobacco crop in Rhodesia.

FRUITS AND PREPARATIONS   Exports of fruits and preparations last year were the second highest on record. Exports of fruits and preparations in fiscal year 1959-60 are estimated at $246 million compared with $229 million in 1958-59. Last year's exports were only 6 percent smaller than the record of $262 million in 1957-58. Principal increases were in fresh apples, fresh oranges, dried prunes, raisins, and canned fruits. The expansion of exports was brought about primarily by ample supplies in the United States, prosperous conditions in Western Europe, and some dollar liberalization.

VEGETABLES AND PREPARATIONS   Exports of vegetables and preparations as a group were helped by record shipments of dried beans. Exports of vegetables and preparations in fiscal year 1959-60, estimated at $146 million, were 8 percent above the $135 million a year earlier. Major items were fresh and canned vegetables and dried beans and peas. Dried bean exports are estimated at a record 390 million pounds for 1959-60 compared with 341 million in the previous fiscal year. Dried pea exports, estimated at 210 million pounds, were the highest in over a decade. The heavy exports of beans and peas reflected reduced crops in Europe and Latin America.

ANIMALS AND   Exports of major animal products were up in fiscal year
ANIMAL PRODUCTS 1959-60. Exports of animals and animal products, in-
                cluding USDA donations, are estimated at $582 million in
fiscal year 1959-60, 9 percent ahead of the $533 million in 1958-59. Ship-
ments of lard, tallow, poultry meats, and variety meats were stimulated
last year by plentiful U. S. supplies and relatively low prices. While
total exports of dairy products last year declined considerably, exports
other than USDA donations were one-fifth larger. Egg exports were somewhat less.

Both lard and tallow exports gained substantially last year, with tallow
setting a new record. Tallow exports in fiscal year 1959-60, at an estimated 1,598 million pounds, were 43 percent larger than the 1,196 million
a year earlier. Exports were encouraged by ample U. S. supplies at competitive prices, reflecting increased slaughter of cattle at heavier
weights. Foreign markets, which took about half of U. S. output, were
principally Italy, Japan, and the Netherlands. Lard exports of an estimated 660 million pounds were the second largest since World War II. The
United Kingdom was the major foreign outlet. Increased hog slaughter
resulted in plentiful supplies at reduced prices. In addition, shipping
most of the lard in tankers reduced the price in the foreign market by
about 10 percent.

                    I M P O R T   H I G H L I G H T S

July-May agricultural imports showed little change from a year earlier.
July-May agricultural imports in 1959-60 totaled $3,671 million, slightly
higher than the $3,667 million in 1958-59. An increase in complementary
(noncompetitive) imports of $45 million more than offset a decline in sup-
plementary (competitive) imports of $42 million. Major complementary gain
was in crude rubber, followed by smaller increases in silk, bananas,
spices, and tea. There were value reductions in coffee and cocoa beans.
Among the supplementary products, increases in beef and veal, hides and
skins, copra, and fresh tomatoes were canceled by declines in live cattle,
pork, feeds and fodders, and vegetable oils. For the year ending June 30,
1960, imports are likely to equal those of the previous year--$4 billion--
and to be about evenly divided between supplementary and complementary
commodities.

Both supplementary and complementary imports were lower in May. Both
groups totaled $342 million in May 1960, 5 percent lower than in May 1959.
Supplementary imports alone, valued at $181 million, were $4 million below
a year earlier. The declines in dutiable cattle, apparel wool, and beef
and veal exceeded the increases in cane sugar, nuts and preparations, and
tomatoes. Complementary imports meanwhile totaled $161 million in May
1960, $15 million less than in May 1959. Value declines in coffee, carpet
wool, and rubber accounted for the decrease.

July-May imports of beef, veal, and mutton increased in 1959-60. A decline in the domestic slaughter of low grade cattle during the past 2 years
with a resultant sharp rise in prices of low grade meat has encouraged imports of boneless and canned beef. July-May beef and veal imports rose

- Continued on page 8 -

DOMESTIC EXPORTS: May 1959 and 1960 and July-May 1958-59 and 1959-60 1/

Commodity exported	Unit	May Quantity 1959	May Quantity 1960	May Value 2/ 1959 (1,000 dollars)	May Value 2/ 1960 (1,000 dollars)	July-May Quantity 1958-59 (Thousands)	July-May Quantity 1959-60 (Thousands)	July-May Value 2/ 1958-59 (1,000 dollars)	July-May Value 2/ 1959-60 (1,000 dollars)
		Thousands	Thousands						
Cheese*	lb.	877	689	316	327	50,351	13,921	14,191	5,564
Evaporated milk*	lb.	4,525	5,932	688	946	96,725	87,410	15,404	13,587
Dried who e milk	lb.	1,535	2,787	854	1,378	23,191	29,259	11,856	15,381
Nonfat dry milk*	lb.	110,538	29,489	9,659	3,716	636,848	404,520	68,762	43,020
Eggs, in the shell	Doz.	1,275	460	878	1,020	27,077	19,656	14,707	11,308
Hides and skins 3/	No.	863	795	7,229	6,043	7,823	7,952	49,901	64,074
Beef and veal, total 4/	lb.	2,283	2,062	915	799	22,805	27,592	9,168	0,690
Pork, total 4/	lb.	5,709	5,948	748	2,144	54,869	69,922	18,716	20,215
Variety meats 5/	lb.	7,420	7,986	1,569	1,580	78,642	96,151	18,655	18,893
Poultry, canned, fresh or frozen 4/	lb.	8,718	10,746	2,556	3,065	69,795	138,527	21,993	37,648
Lard	lb.	45,63	49,825	4,830	4,678	419,036	610,876	50,610	55,939
Tallow, edib e and inedible	lb.	96,169	139,646	7,790	9,180	1,013,096	1,457,788	84,734	101,830
Cotton, unmfd., excl. linters (running bales)	Bale	248	524	30,585	69,97 66	2,893	6,135	383,414	760,800
Apples, fresh	lb.	7,053	7,883	543	66	106,824	174,908	8,738	14,293
Oranges and tangerines, fresh	lb.	65,73	56,848	4,357	4,077	431,100	478,386	31,615	34,122
Prunes, dried	lb.	2,174	2,784	574	664	61,297	72,478	14,085	17,255
Raisins and currants	lb.	1,289	3,102	373	438	43,229	79,276	10,853	12,946
Fruits, canned 6/	lb.	12,388	21,385	2,075	3,181	256,743	313,331	39,882	44,305
Orange juice	Gal.	1,130	1,331	2,382	2,036	11,080	12,659	21,480	21,184
Barley, grain (48 lb.)	Bu.	3,956	3,613	4,366	3,912	00,571	101,975	114,509	107,941
Corn, grain (56 lb.)*	Bu.	21,451	15,289	28,616	20,469	183,800	194,116	241,416	252,425
Gra h sorghums (56 lb.)	Bu.	6,849	8,292	8,261	9,322	87,814	94,027	103,591	104,784
Oats, grain (32 lb.)	Bu.	2,183	637	1,606	493	25,618	38,642	18,241	28,316
Rice, mi ed, excludes paddy*	lb.	142,743	194,157	8,853	12,570	1,228,552	1,849,99	89,563	124,750
Rye, gra h (56 lb.)	Bu.	285	489	388	693	8,329	4,465	10,317	5,722
Wheat, grain (60 lb.)*	Bu.	36,902	47,240	63,96	81,665	334,691	380,981	577,315	646,614
Flour, who ly of U. S. wheat (100 lb.)*	Bu.	3,615	2,617	14,99	10,602	31,218	36,580	136,711	150,147
Oil cake and oil-cake meal (2,000 lb.)	Ton	26	38	1,762	2,544	441	820	28,636	53,933
Flaxseed (56 lb.)	Bu.	244	129	712	360	5,158	7,760	15,196	24,958
Soybeans, except canned (60 lb.)	Bu.	9,219	4,129	21,751	32,624	93,948	120,156	217,272	273,714
Soybean oil, crude, refined, etc.	lb.	5,68	109,760	12,924	10,860	742,193	868,565	93,274	92,805
Cottonseed oil, crude, refined, etc.	lb.	52,938	27,8 5	6,460	2,989	259,530	550,750	32,367	67,745
Tobacco, unmanufactured	lb.	24,951	23,437	18,882	17,654	447,510	427,074	331,638	3 9,607
Beans, dried*	lb.	54,977	40,389	4,335	3,207	294,733	349,076	23,30	27,694
Peas, dr ed (except cowpeas and chickpeas)	lb.	6,423	12,154	466	752	143,539	198,403	9,338	12,736
Potatoes, white	lb.	29,942	57,114	880	1,99	254,357	306,710	6,444	9,057
Vegetables, canned 6/	lb.	7,369	7,115	863	1,092	86,234	82,653	12,738	12,581
Other agricultural commodities				45,478	44,829			463,367	524,778
TOTAL AGRICULTURAL COMMODITIES				325,029	373,521			3,414,867	4,143,361
TOTAL NONAGRICULTURAL COMMODITIES				1,210,233	1,402,048			12,458,746	13,156,616
TOTAL ALL COMMODITIES				1,535,262	1,775,569			15,873,613	17,299,977

1/ Preliminary. 2/ At place of export. 3/ Excludes the weight of "other hides and skins", reported in value only. 4/ Product weight. 5/ Includes beef and pork livers, beef tongues, and other variety meats, fresh or frozen. Product weight. 6/ Includes only classes shown separately in Table 2 of the monthly "Foreign Agricultural Trade".
* Includes "Food exported for relief or charity by individuals and private agencies".

Compiled from official records, Bureau of the Census.

IMPORTS (FOR CONSUMPTION): May 1959 and 1960 and July-May 1958-59 and 1959-60 1/

Commodity Imported	Unit	May Quantity 1959 (Thousands)	May Quantity 1960 (Thousands)	May Value 1959 (1,000 dollars)	May Value 1960 (1,000 dollars)	July-May Quantity 1958-59 (Thousands)	July-May Quantity 1959-60 (Thousands)	July-May Value 1958-59 (1,000 dollars)	July-May Value 1959-60 (1,000 dollars)
SUPPLEMENTARY									
Cattle, dutiable	No.	95	76	12,068	6,919	995	592	118,465	61,138
Casein or lactarene	Lb.	6,146	7,565	1,056	1,414	85,601	80,295	16,145	15,618
Cheese	Lb.	4,268	4,670	2,061	2,059	53,967	56,894	25,587	28,071
Hides and skins	Lb.	18,728	16,201	7,591	7,571	161,883	144,787	63,569	71,528
Beef and veal, total 2/	Lb.	43,688	36,220	15,957	13,247	470,689	550,528	167,978	192,733
Pork, total 2/	Lb.	15,689	14,646	9,477	8,607	180,224	148,110	118,223	97,735
Mutton, goat and lamb, fresh or frozen 2/	Lb.	5,596	3,706	1,420	771	38,109	48,907	9,576	10,415
Sausage casings	Lb.	1,226	1,132	920	926	13,861	13,472	11,106	10,042
Wool unmfd., excl. free, etc. (actual weight)	Lb.	15,813	7,429	9,705	5,883	136,461	122,749	88,237	87,874
Cotton, unmfd., e cxl linters (480 lb.)	Bale	4	1	343	126	135	143	24,651	21,430
Jute and jute butts, unmfd. (2,240 lb.)	Ton	7	6	1,379	889	41	70	8,436	11,213
Olives in brine	Gal.	1,168	1,585	1,803	1,890	12,084	13,168	8,343	17,543
Pineapples, canned, prepared or preserved	Lb.	6,577	7,325	768	903	72,228	98,258	8,344	11,433
Barley, grain (48 lb.)	Bu.	609	1,113	779	1,513	10,305	13,626	13,691	17,889
Oats, grain (32 lb.)	Bu.	146	101	156	116	3,167	1,735	2,781	1,831
Wheat, grain (60 lb.)	Bu.	359	388	583	644	7,275	6,412	11,281	10,526
Feeds and fodders		3/	3/	1,095	405	3/	3/	14,332	7,284
Nuts and preparations				4,332	6,125			59,620	63,317
Copra	Lb.	66,217	69,922	6,898	6,627	571,120	654,513	51,753	61,636
Vegetable oils, fats, and waxes, expressed	Lb.	51,050	39,414	9,801	7,577	496,140	467,386	88,077	83,807
Seeds, field and garden		3/	3/	954	821	3/		11,460	17,906
Sugar, cane (2,000 lb.)	Ton	477	545	51,476	58,305	4,116	4,233	452,314	456,191
Molasses, unf k for human consumption	Gal.	28,218	58,352	3,142	4,609	283,963	327,776	33,030	29,993
Tobacco, unmanufactured	Lb.	13,306	13,062	9,899	9,768	139,367	142,307	103,349	104,646
Tomatoes, natural state	Lb.	7,854	24,061	697	2,041	236,394	306,169	17,562	23,374
Other supplementary				30,410	31,137			310,816	291,931
Total supplementary				184,715	180,893			1,848,626	1,807,104
COMPLEMENTARY									
Silk, raw	Lb.	760	395	2,854	1,615	4,812	6,363	16,662	25,228
Wool, unmfd., free in bond (actual weight)	Lb.	23,557	13,788	11,336	7,912	216,503	191,393	99,176	103,593
Bananas	Bunch	4,324	5,537	6,623	7,812	45,598	51,445	65,629	72,359
Cocoa or cacao beans	Lb.	46,834	68,078	16,497	16,739	405,116	458,834	150,369	136,152
Coffee (incl. into Puerto Rico)	Lb.	249,010	240,200	93,049	82,329	2,635,928	2,751,161	1,028,149	962,501
Coffee essences, substitutes, etc.	Lb.	358	382	733	640	4,250	4,259	9,153	7,497
Tea	Lb.	10,071	10,588	4,519	5,159	99,722	106,269	46,652	51,554
Spices (complementary)	Lb.	6,554	6,866	2,766	3,939	78,769	88,121	31,881	40,629
Abaca or Manila (2,240 lb.)	Ton	10	2	1,610	1,275	42	27	14,186	13,233
Sisal and henequen (2,240 lb.)	Ton	10	6	1,389	1,100	112	100	16,852	16,809
Rubber, crude	Lb.	101,808	71,720	28,362	26,815	1,097,843	1,047,998	273,005	355,716
Other complementary				6,153	6,082			66,869	78,722
Total complementary				175,891	161,417			1,818,583	1,863,993
TOTAL AGRICULTURAL COMMODITIES				360,606	342,310			3,667,209	3,671,097
TOTAL NONAGRICULTURAL COMMODITIES				886,679	910,824			8,892,426	10,329,266
TOTAL ALL COMMODITIES				1,247,285	1,253,134			12,559,635	14,000,363

1/ Preliminary. 2/ Product weight. 3/ Reported in value only.

Compiled from official records, Bureau of the Census.

- 8 -

- Continued from page 5 -

from 471 million pounds (product weight) in 1958-59 to 551 million in
1959-60. Monthly imports after December 1959 tended to run behind a year
earlier. Mutton imports rose as the result of a strong demand for this
product as a substitute for low grade beef in the manufacture of frank-
furters. July-May imports of fresh and frozen mutton, goat, and lamb increased from 38 million pounds in 1958-59 to 49 million in 1959-60; however, April-May imports in 1960 were smaller than in 1959.

Fewer cattle and less pork were imported in 1959-60. Imports of dutiable
cattle dropped sharply as stronger demand in both Mexico and Canada, our
leading suppliers, left fewer animals available for export. July-May
dutiable cattle imports fell from 995 thousand head in 1958-59 to 592
thousand in 1959-60. Increased U. S. hog slaughter resulted in a decline
in pork imports from 180 million to 148 million pounds.

Wool imports declined as world prices increased. July-May wool imports
decreased in volume from 1958-59 to 1959-60 as world wool prices advanced
to higher levels. All of the $5 million value rise occurred in carpet
wool. Carpet wool imports declined in volume from 216 million pounds
(actual weight) to 191 million, and apparel wool imports declined from
136 million pounds to 123 million. U. S. woolen manufacturers have
drawn heavily on accumulated wool stocks purchased at lower prices.

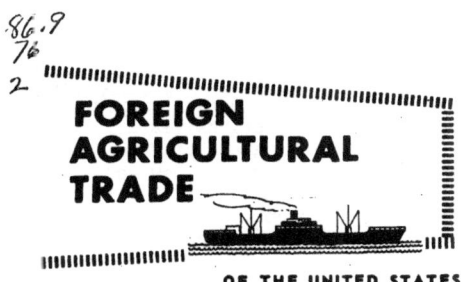

FOREIGN AGRICULTURAL TRADE

OF THE UNITED STATES

Digest

SEPTEMBER 1960

Issued monthly by Foreign Agricultural Service, United States Department of Agriculture, Washington 25, D.C. Free within U.S. on request. Also available are monthly and yearly Foreign Agricultural Trade Statistical Reports, containing detailed statistics on quantity and value of exports and imports.

EXPORT HIGHLIGHTS

Agricultural exports in July were 9 percent ahead of a year earlier. July exports totaled $359 million in 1960 compared with $328 million in 1959. Cotton was the principal commodity to show a substantial increase, reflecting largely the increased foreign consumption and replenishment of low stocks abroad. Other major exports which were larger in July included wheat and flour and rice. Declines occurred in vegetable oils and oilseeds, feed grains, and tobacco. Exports of animals and animal products, fruits, and vegetables remained close to year-earlier levels.

U. S. agricultural exports,
by commodity, fiscal year

Commodity	1958-59 1/	1959-60	Chg.
	Million dollars		Pct.
Cotton	413	826	+100
Grains & feeds 2/	1,523	1,702	+12
Wheat & flour 2/	776	875	+13
Feed grains 2/ 3/	527	543	+3
Rice, milled 2/	104	136	+31
Tobacco, unmfd.	350	342	-2
Veg. oils & seeds	425	546	+28
Soybeans	238	303	+27
Ed. veg. oils 4/	136	178	+31
Fruits & preps.	229	250	+9
Vegs. & preps. 2/	135	150	+11
Animals & prods. 2/	533	583	+9
Fats & oils	159	185	+16
Meats & prods.	94	113	+20
Hides & skins	55	69	+25
Dairy products 2/	144	127	-12
Other 2/	111	128	+15
Total	3,719	4,527	+22

1/ Partly revised. 2/ Includes private relief. 3/ Excludes products. 4/ Cottonseed and soybean.

Actual exports in fiscal year 1960 totaled $4,527 million. This total was 22 percent above the $3,719 million in the previous year. This level--second highest on record--was only $201 million less than the record of $4,728 million in fiscal year 1957. All principal commodity groups, except tobacco, were larger last year than in 1958-59. (For latest data see tables on this page and on page 6; for detailed analysis, see previous issue.)

Sales for dollars in 1960 were the second highest on record. Last year's $0.8 billion increase in U. S. agricultural exports was largely the result of expanded sales for dollars inasmuch as Government-financed-program shipments increased only negligibly. Dollar exports expanded from $2.4 billion in fiscal year 1959 to $3.2 billion in 1960. Last year's exports for dollars were only $200 million less than in the record year 1952.

Government-financed export programs accounted for 29 percent of fiscal year 1960 shipments. Exports under Public Law 480 and Mutual Security programs totaled $1,300 million, about the same as in the two previous years. Exports increased under Title I, Title II, and barter programs of Public Law 480 and declined under the welfare donation program of Public Law 480 and the Mutual Security program. Wheat and flour exports accounted for 50 percent of Government-financed exports; feed grains, 13 percent; cotton, 12 percent; vegetable oils and oilseeds, 9 percent; rice, 6 percent; tobacco, 5 percent; and other commodities, 5 percent.

Over two-thirds of last year's exports went to 14 countries. The value of U. S. exports to these countries ranged from $475 million for the United Kingdom to $74 million for the Republic of Korea. The five best markets--the United Kingdom, Japan, Canada, West Germany, and the Netherlands--accounted for over half of the value gain last year. The top five each took over $300 million of U. S. farm products, and all were important dollar markets. The other countries which took more U. S. farm products included India, Italy, Belgium, France, UAR-Egypt, Poland, and Venezuela. Declines occurred in exports to Cuba and the Republic of Korea.

IMPORT HIGHLIGHTS

Agricultural imports were slightly larger in 1960. U. S. agricultural imports for consumption totaled $4,017 million in fiscal year 1960 compared with $4,004 million a year earlier. Imports last year were the sixth highest on record. In the past 5 years they have been remarkably stable, with values ranging from $3.8 billion in 1956-57 to $4.1 billion in 1955-56. Relatively strong domestic demand for some commodities, especially livestock and meats, and the continued high level of U. S. economic activity were the main factors in the continuing stability of agricultural imports.

U. S. agricultural exports by country of destination, fiscal year

Country	1958-59	1959-60	Change
	Million dollars		Pct.
United Kingdom	399	475	+19
Japan	317	441	+39
Canada	355	410	+15
West Germany	274	374	+36
Netherlands	242	339	+40
India	251	279	+11
Italy	106	155	+46
Belgium	105	134	+27
Cuba	144	125	-13
France	65	119	+83
Egypt	36	95	+164
Venezuela	87	95	+9
Poland	59	93	+58
Korea	80	74	-7
Other	1,199	1,319	+10
Total	3,719	4,527	+22

Supplementary imports declined last year. Imports of supplementary products--items similar to or interchangeable with those of U. S. agriculture--fell from $2,029 million in 1959 to $1,982 million in 1960. Declines in imports of dutiable cattle and pork accounted for a considerable drop in supplementary imports, but there were substantial gains in beef and veal, hides and skins, and vegetable oils.

Small rise in complementary imports offset supplementary decline. Imports of complementary (noncompetitive) products increased from $1,975 million in 1959 to $2,035 million in 1960. The $81 million gain in imports of crude natural

TRADE NEWS ROUNDUP

U. S. voluntary relief agencies will have 180 million pounds of rice and up to 500 million pounds of nonfat dry milk available for foreign donation this fiscal year, according to an announcement by Secretary Benson at a Food-for-Peace Conference of U. S. Voluntary Agencies, in Washington, D. C., September 1. Twenty agencies and the United Nations Children's Fund are currently donating nonfat dry milk, flour, cornmeal, and rice to more than 60 million needy persons in 90 countries and territories. Donations of surplus foods since 1953 have totaled nearly 9 billion pounds costing $1½ billion (70 percent dairy products).

————————O————————

Agricultural implications of U. S.-Cuban relations are indicated by the fact that last year Cuba was the sixth largest cash customer for U. S. farm products--taking $132 million worth, mainly pork, pork products, and grains. Cuba is orienting its predominantly Government-controlled trade towards the Sino-Soviet Bloc. A recent commercial pact with Communist China guarantees the annual purchase of 500,000 tons of Cuban sugar for 5 years. Cuba is also trying to become self-sufficient in food.

————————O————————

U. S. agriculture continues to go after the big food-importing markets of Western Europe. This month USDA and U. S. agricultural groups are jointly sponsoring promotional exhibits of U. S. foods at London and Munich. London is the scene of the biennial British Food Fair, September 1-17; Munich, the IKOFA International Exhibition of Groceries and High Class Provisions, September 23-October 2. Products being promoted include wheat, rice, honey, meat, poultry, lard, soybeans, fruit, nonfat dry milk, canned soups, prepared food mixes, and processed packaged foods.

————————O————————

Title I Public Law 480 agreements announced since July 25: ...Iran: $3.7 million for wheat. ...India: $41.6 million for cotton (supplemental agreement. ...UAR-Egypt: $58.2 million for wheat or flour. ...UAR-Syria: $17 million for wheat or flour. ...Chile: $300 thousand for corn. ...Taiwan: $14.2 million for wheat or flour, vegetable oil, cotton, and tobacco.

————————O————————

The U. S. livestock and meat industry, which already has a good market from Dutch traders who transship to other countries, may soon develop a market in the Netherlands itself. On July 1 the Netherlands removed restrictions on imports for consumption of pork, bacon, and live hogs (other than pedigreed breeding stock) from all member countries of the General Agreement on Tariffs and Trade, including the United States.

————————O————————

Colombia's recent purchase of 746 head of U. S. breeding sheep represented the largest shipment since 1946. Colombia does not produce enough wool for its needs and is developing its sheep and wool industry.

rubber more than accounted for the total gain of $60 million. Other increases were in spices, raw silk, carpet wool, bananas, and tea. Value declines reflecting lower prices occurred in coffee, cocoa beans, and hard fibers.

SUPPLEMENTARY IMPORTS   Imports of dutiable cattle declined by 430 thousand head in fiscal year 1960. Dutiable cattle imports,which have been over 1 million head in the past 2 years, fell to 629 million in 1960. This substantial drop is attributed to the larger U. S. supplies and lower prices of feeder-type cattle and increased Canadian prices for feeder cattle.

Small marketings of manufacturing-type beef and veal encouraged imports. Imports of beef and veal rose from 527 million pounds in 1959 to 593 million in 1960. U. S. production of processing and manufacturing meats in the past 2 or 3 years has been relatively low as U. S. farmers and ranchers held back culling their cattle in order to build up herds.

Imports of pork declined as U. S. production increased last year. Imports of pork declined from 196 million pounds in 1959 to 166 million in 1960. Most of the decline was in fresh, chilled, and frozen pork from Canada. The United States depended less on imports of pork as U. S. production increased by 10 percent. Over two-thirds of the imported pork consisted of canned hams and shoulders which have a stable market in the United States and generally sell at higher prices than corresponding domestic products.

Imports of hides and skins declined due to reduced demand. Hides and skins imports of 160 million pounds in 1960 were 11 percent below the 184 million a year earlier. Factors contributing to the decline were a drop in domestic demand in the second half and higher foreign prices in the first half of fiscal year 1960.

Imports of apparel wool also declined in 1960. Apparel wool imports totaled 133 million pounds in 1960 compared with 148 million a year earlier. This decline reflected the drawing on inventories of wool stocks, a leveling off in consumption, a continued rise in domestic output, and higher world prices. During 1959, when world prices were relatively low, manufacturers increased imports to build up stocks and to meet rapidly expanding demand. Following a price spurt at the end of fiscal 1959 and with the upturn in mill use slowing down, stocks were reduced in 1960.

Sugar imports were record high in fiscal year 1960. Imports of cane sugar rose from 4.6 million short tons in 1959 to 4.7 million in 1960, a new record. Cuba shipped a greater proportion of its quota earlier this season than a year ago. Some countries were able to ship more sugar to the United States because of an adjustment in the sugar quota owing to the deficit in some of the U. S. production areas.

Increased cigarette consumption required more foreign tobacco. Imports of unmanufactured tobacco increased from 152 million pounds in 1959 to 157 million in 1960, a new record. U. S. cigarette manufacturers increased output over 1959 and used more oriental-type leaf in their blends.

- Continued on page 8 -

DOMESTIC EXPORTS: July 1959 and 1960 1/

Commodity exported	Unit	July			
		Quantity		Value 2/	
		1959	1960	1959	1960
		Thousands	Thousands	1,000 dollars	1,000 dollars
Cheese*	Lb.	638	732	271	352
Evaporated milk*	Lb.	17,073	14,038	2,638	2,232
Dried whole milk	Lb.	2,560	2,401	1,399	1,448
Nonfat dry milk*	Lb.	74,629	55,075	7,617	6,249
Eggs, in the shell	Doz.	1,164	1,969	765	1,036
Hides and skins 3/	No.	611	891	5,610	6,088
Beef and veal, total 4/	Lb.	2,095	1,770	828	729
Pork, total 4/	Lb.	5,788	3,006	1,606	973
Variety meats 5/	Lb.	7,487	8,143	1,588	1,810
Poultry, canned, fresh or frozen 4/ .	Lb.	10,364	10,683	2,847	3,083
Lard	Lb.	58,365	42,940	5,601	4,366
Tallow, edible and inedible	Lb.	115,015	131,744	8,753	8,637
Cotton, unmfd., excl. linters (running bales)	Bale	129	676	15,432	86,359
Apples, fresh	Lb.	3,893	4,840	289	405
Oranges and tangerines, fresh	Lb.	60,976	48,980	4,320	3,502
Prunes, dried	Lb.	1,270	4,193	336	1,040
Raisins and currants	Lb.	1,556	2,865	405	418
Fruits, canned 6/	Lb.	21,844	16,503	3,271	2,558
Orange juice	Gal.	821	1,053	1,672	1,931
Barley, grain (48 lb.)	Bu.	13,943	5,717	13,614	5,972
Corn, grain (56 lb.)*	Bu.	22,472	15,881	29,117	20,550
Grain sorghums (56 lb.)	Bu.	8,091	9,687	8,818	10,853
Oats, grain (32 lb.)	Bu.	9,126	1,991	5,930	1,514
Rice, milled, excludes paddy*	Lb.	143,015	152,529	9,333	9,909
Rye, grain (56 lb.)	Bu.	433	1,007	558	982
Wheat, grain (60 lb.)*	Bu.	33,981	37,571	58,150	64,233
Flour, wholly of U.S. wheat (100 lb)*	Bag	2,451	2,383	11,318	10,397
Oil cake and oil-cake meal (2,000 lb)	Ton	45	38	3,099	2,431
Flaxseed (56 lb.)	Bu.	2,349	628	7,280	2,008
Soybeans, except canned (60 lb.)	Bu.	9,850	9,210	23,193	21,369
Soybean oil, crude, refined, etc. ...	Lb.	155,386	80,582	18,140	8,560
Cottonseed oil, crude, refined etc. .	Lb.	66,414	27,836	10,587	3,218
Tobacco, unmanufactured	Lb.	23,070	20,560	16,754	14,674
Beans, dried*	Lb.	52,461	23,258	4,078	1,793
Peas, dried (ex. cowpeas & chickpeas)	Lb.	5,159	10,971	297	595
Potatoes, white	Lb.	25,272	47,898	801	1,222
Vegetables, canned 6/	Lb.	8,094	10,065	1,282	1,539
Other agricultural commodities				40,156	43,542
TOTAL AGRICULTURAL COMMODITIES .				327,753	358,577
TOTAL NONAGRICULTURAL COMM.				1,126,198	1,323,822
TOTAL ALL COMMODITIES				1,453,951	1,682,399

1/ Preliminary. 2/ At place of export. 3/ Excludes the weight of "other hides and skins", reported in value only. 4/ Product weight. 5/ Includes beef and pork livers, beef tongues, and other variety meats, fresh or frozen. Product weight. 6/ Includes only classes shown separately in Table 2 of the monthly "Foreign Agricultural Trade".
* Includes "Food exported for relief or charity by individuals and private agencies".

Compiled from official records, Bureau of the Census.

DOMESTIC EXPORTS: June 1959 and 1960 and July-June 1958-59 and 1959-60 1/

Commodity exported	Unit	June Quantity 1959 (Thousands)	June Quantity 1960 (Thousands)	June Value 2/ 1959 (1,000 dollars)	June Value 2/ 1960 (1,000 dollars)	July-June Quantity 1958-59 (Thousands)	July-June Quantity 1959-60 (Thousands)	July-June Value 2/ 1958-59 (1,000 dollars)	July-June Value 2/ 1959-60 (1,000 dollars)
Cheese*	Lb.	722	633	311	288	51,073	14,554	14,502	5,851
Evaporated ml k*	Lb.	5,983	9,386	860	1,518	102,708	96,797	16,264	15,104
Dried whole ml k	Lb.	2,203	2,525	1,258	1,493	25,394	31,703	13,114	16,833
Nonfat dry milk*	Lb.	69,991	56,400	6,315	7,554	706,839	463,587	75,077	51,059
Eggs, in the shell 3/	Doz.	1,064	937	718	704	28,141	20,593	15,426	12,013
Hides and skins 3/	No.	657	760	5,427	5,223	8,479	8,712	55,328	69,297
Beef and veal, total 4/	Lb.	1,759	2,142	751	874	24,563	29,734	9,919	11,564
Pork, total 4/	Lb.	4,801	3,583	1,615	1,264	59,670	73,505	20,330	21,478
Variety meats 5/	Lb.	4,780	8,137	1,102	1,724	83,423	104,288	19,757	20,618
Poultry, canned, fresh or frozen 4/	Lb.	11,576	0,362	3,327	2,838	81,371	148,917	25,320	40,501
Lard	Lb.	46,840	62,724	4,735	6,041	465,876	673,600	55,345	61,980
Tallow, edible and inedible	Lb.	103,387	112,527	8,250	7,493	1,116,483	1,568,727	92,984	109,225
Cotton, unmfd., e cxl linters (running bales)	Bale	236	501	29,324	64,871	3,129	6,636	412,737	825,671
App es] fresh	Lb.	5,899	2,807	408	264	112,723	177,715	9,146	14,558
Oranges and tangerines, fresh	Lb.	68,296	58,54	4,811	4,430	499,396	536,540	36,425	38,552
Prunes, dried	Lb.	1,535	3,375	408	826	62,832	75,853	14,494	18,081
Raisins and currants	Lb.	1,618	2,915	427	452	44,847	82,191	11,280	13,398
Fruits, canned 6/	Lb.	19,214	17,323	3,087	2, 69	275,957	330,653	42, 69	47,004
Orange juice	Gal.	991	1,497	2,127	2,354	12,071	14,156	23, 67	23,537
Barley, grain (48 lb.)	Bu.	11,663	4,423	12,006	4,583	112,234	114,240	126,515	120,160
Corn, grain (56 lb.)*	Bu.	19,687	16,168	26,247	21,229	203,656	216,258	267,896	280,692
Grain sorghums (56 lb.)	Bu.	6,761	4,814	7,416	5,527	94,575	98,841	111,007	110,311
Oats, grain (32 lb.)	Bu.	4,217	192	2,840	219	29,835	43,402	21,081	32,028
Rice, milled, excludes paddy*	Lb.	173,444	173,374	11, 69	11,474	1,401,996	2,023,173	101,232	136,224
Rye, grain (56 lb.)	Bu.	136	158	155	203	8,465	5,266	10,472	6,703
Wheat, gra h (60 lb.)*	Bu.	26,852	34,842	45,811	57,684	361,543	420,376	623,126	711,965
Flour, wholly of U. S. wheat (100 lb.)*	Bag	3,808	2,907	15,127	12,614	35,025	39,488	151,838	162,761
Oil cake and oil-cake mea [2,000 lb.)	Ton	38	47	2,591	3,019	479	867	31,228	56,953
Flaxseed (56 lb.)	Bu.	847	256	2,508	850	6,005	8,326	17,704	26,861
Soybeans, except canned (60 lb.)	Bu.	8,880	11,185	21,071	25, 2	102,829	132,981	238,343	302,517
Soybean oil, crude, refined, etc.	Lb.	53,332	171,143	6,722	16,185	795,525	1,039,709	99, 96	108,990
Cottonseed oil, crude, refined, etc.	Lb.	25,424	10,120	4,117	1,152	284,954	560,870	36,484	68,897
Tobacco, unmanufactured	Lb.	25,777	29,574	18,574	22,244	473,288	456,647	350,212	341,851
Beans, dried*	Lb.	47,953	37,016	3,786	2,810	342,685	386,092	27,356	30,504
Peas, dr ell (except cowpeas and chickpeas)	Lb.	9,374	13,311	636	774	152,913	211,714	9,974	13,510
Potatoes, white	Lb.	51,942	96,137	2,061	2, 69	306,300	402,846	8, 66	11, 66
Vegetables, canned 6/	Lb.	9,298	15,292	1,512	2,615	95,532	97,945	14,250	15,196
Other agricultural commodities				44,145	47,768			508,111	572,946
TOTAL AGRICULTURAL COMMODITIES				304,255	351,680			3,719,355	4,527,059
TOTAL NONAGRICULTURAL COMMODITIES				1,105,270	1,351,557			13,563,783	14,476,155
TOTAL ALL COMMODITIES				1,409,525	1,703,237			17,283,138	19,003,214

1/ Preliminary. 2/ At place of export. 3/ Excludes the weight of "other hides and skins", reported in value only. 4/ Product weight. 5/ Includes beef and pork livers, beef tongues, and other variety meats, fresh or frozen. Product weight. 6/ Includes only classes shown separately in Table 2 of the monthly "Foreign Agricultural Trade".
* Includes "Food exported for relief or charity by individuals and private agencies".

Compiled from official records, Bureau of the Census.

IMPORTS (FOR CONSUMPTION): June 1959 and 1960 and July-June 1958-59 and 1959-60 1/

Commodity imported	Units	June Quantity (Thousands) 1959	June Quantity (Thousands) 1960	June Value (1,000 dollars) 1959	June Value (1,000 dollars) 1960	July-June Quantity (Thousands) 1958-59	July-June Quantity (Thousands) 1959-60	July-June Value (1,000 dollars) 1958-59	July-June Value (1,000 dollars) 1959-60
SUPPLEMENTARY									
Catt e] dutiable	No.	64	37	9,203	4,019	1,059	629	127,668	65,162
Casein or lactarene	lb.	12,395	13,103	2,318	2,648	97,996	93,398	18,463	18,466
Se	lb.	5,148	4,494	2,357	2,165	59,115	61,388	27,944	30,236
Hides and skins	lb.	21,642	15,766	8,759	7,798	183,524	160,454	72,328	79,326
Beef and veal, total 2/	lb.	56,785	43,044	20,283	15,532	527,474	593,460	188,260	208,230
Pork, total 2/	lb.	15,705	17,329	10,284	11,392	195,930	166,019	128,507	109,618
Mutton, goat and lamb, fresh or frozen 2/	lb.	6,852	3,716	1,627	756	44,962	52,623	11,203	11,121
Sausage casings	lb.	1,223	1,400	705	1,335	15,085	14,872	11,712	11,377
Woo ½ umfd., excl. free, etc.. (actual weight)	lb.	11,792	10,370	6,890	6,997	148,218	133,105	95,108	94,861
Cotton, unmfd., e cxl interb (480 lb.)	Bale	2	2	222	190	137	145	24,873	21,620
Jute and jute butts, unmfd. (2,240 lb.)	Ton	7	3	826	456	48	74	9,262	11,668
Olives in brine	Gal.	1,243	1,257	1,916	1,493	13,327	14,425	20,259	19,036
Pineapples, canned, prepared or preserved	lb.	11,881	18,820	1,375	2,087	84,109	7,078	9,719	13,520
Barley, gra h (48 lb.)	Bu.	689	640	925	842	10,995	14,266	14,616	18,731
Oats, grain (32 lb.)	Bu.	98	74	103	83	3,265	1,809	2,883	1,914
Wheat, grain (60 lb.)	Bu.	774	1,858	1,234	2,961	8,049	8,150	12,515	13,309
Feeds and fodders	3/	3/	3/	1,170	369	3/	3/	15,502	7,653
Nuts and preparations	lb.	3/	3/	5,082	6,204	3/	3/	64,702	69,520
Copra	lb.	51,998	69,708	5,449	5,919	623,117	724,222	57,203	67,555
Vegetable o s} fats, and wa as, expressed	lb.	43,677	56,582	7,927	5,405	539,806	523,967	95,997	93,263
Seeds, f e H and garden	3/	3/	3/	872	537	3/	3/	12,332	18,446
Sugar, cane (2,000 lb.)	Ton	482	461	52,339	49,934	4,598	4,695	504,653	507,479
Molasses, unfit for human consumption	Gal.	25,876	40,313	2,739	2,828	309,839	367,808	35,769	32,788
Tobacco, unmanufactured	lb.	12,671	14,783	8,979	10,562	152,038	157,066	112,328	114,882
Tomatoes, natural state	lb.	430	3,160	29	320	236,824	309,328	17,592	23,694
Other supplementary				26,717	26,242			337,532	318,888
Total supplementary				180,330	173,774			2,028,930	1,982,163
COMPLEMENTARY									
Silk, raw	lb.	432	559	1,649	2,321	5,244	6,922	18,310	27,549
Woo ½ umfd, free in bond (actual weight)	lb.	23,553	21,909	11,858	12,695	240,092	213,312	111,053	116,297
Bananas	Bunch	5,463	5,766	7,406	8,870	51,061	57,211	73,035	81,229
6s or cacao beans	lb.	41,793	70,293	14,864	17,416	446,908	529,127	165,363	153,568
Coffee (incl. into Puerto Rico)	lb.	202,362	251,688	74,215	84,331	2,836,291	3,004,536	1,102,363	1,047,833
Coffee essences, substitutes, etc.	lb.	354	434	790	782	4,604	4,693	9,943	8,279
Tea	lb.	8,983	9,940	4,108	4,824	108,704	116,209	50,760	56,378
Spices (complementary)	lb.	5,747	4,998	2,657	3,328	84,516	93,119	34,538	43,957
Abaca or Manila (2,240 lb.)	Ton	5	7	2,064	586	47	29	16,249	13,820
Sisal and henequen (2,240 lb.)	Ton	11	7	1,786	1,338	123	107	18,638	18,146
Rubber, crude	lb.	103,147	70,871	29,11	26,814	1,200,990	1,119,212	302,116	382,734
Other complementary				5,933	6,338			72,806	85,047
Total complementary				156,441	169,643			1,975,043	2,034,837
TOTAL AGRICULTURAL COMMODITIES				336,771	343,417			4,003,973	4,017,000
TOTAL NONAGRICULTURAL COMMODITIES				998,748	952,156			9,891,182	11,278,937
TOTAL ALL COMMODITIES				1,335,519	1,295,573			13,895,155	15,295,937

1/ Preliminary.   2/ Product weight.   3/ Reported in value only.

Compiled from official records, Bureau of the Census.

- Continued from page   -
- 8 -

Imports of copra increased substantially while those of coconut oil declined.
Imports of copra rose from 623 million pounds in 1959 to 724 million in 1960;
vegetable oils fell from 540 million to 524 million. The drop in vegetable
oils was accounted for by coconut oil. Despite the desire of the Philippines
to ship more coconut oil to world markets, U. S. processors preferred copra
over coconut oil because of the demand for copra cake and meal on the West
Coast. Although the use of coconut oil in soap manufacturing has declined
somewhat in recent years, the demand for this oil for food processing and
industrial uses has increased.

Imports of cotton totaled 145 thousand bales in fiscal year 1960. This
amount was only slightly larger than the 137 thousand bales in the previous
year. With the exception of short, harsh Asiatic cotton, imports are regu-
lated by quotas. The long-staple quota is 95 thousand bales for an August 1-
July 31 year, while the short-staple quota is 30 thousand bales on a
September 20-September 19 year.

Imports of feed grains remained relatively low in 1960. Imports of barley
and wheat, mostly for feed, increased slightly from 1959's low level. Less
oats were imported due to the relatively short world supply. A sharp decline in imports of feeds and fodders, mainly protein meal, reflected the
short supply of cottonseed in Mexico and larger U. S. production of meal.

COMPLEMENTARY IMPORTS   Lower prices stimulated imports of coffee. Imports
                        of coffee totaled 3,005 million pounds in 1960 com-
pared with 2,838 million a year earlier. Plentiful world supplies depressed
prices and caused the value of U. S. imports to drop from $1,102 in 1959 to
$1,048 million in 1960. The relatively low world prices encouraged importers
and processors to build up stocks last year.

Decline in world prices encouraged imports of cocoa beans. Cocoa bean imports increased from 447 million pounds in 1959 to 529 million last year.
However, the value fell from $165 million to $154 million, reflecting the
plentiful world supplies at reduced prices.

Rubber imports declined as prices increased in 1960. Imports of crude
natural rubber totaled 1,119 million pounds in 1960 compared with 1,201 million a year earlier.

286.9
F76
.2

FOREIGN AGRICULTURAL TRADE

OF THE UNITED STATES

Digest

OCTOBER 1960

Issued monthly by Foreign Agricultural Service, United States Department of Agriculture, Washington 25, D.C. Free within U.S. on request. Also available are monthly and yearly Foreign Agricultural Trade Statistical Reports, containing detailed statistics on quantity and value of exports and imports.

EXPORT HIGHLIGHTS

July-August agricultural exports this fiscal year were 9 percent ahead of 1959. Export total was $686 million in July-August 1960 compared with the $632 million in the same period last year. Cotton was the principal item to show a substantial increase this year. Other increases occurred in wheat and soybeans. Exports of vegetable oils, feed grains, and rice fell considerably while those of animal products, tobacco, and fruits and vegetables remained close to last year's high levels.

U. S. agricultural exports, by commodity, July-August

Commodity	1958-59	1959-60	Chg.
	Million dollars		Pct.
Cotton	26	102	+292
Grains & feeds 1/	281	268	-5
Wheat & flour 1/	125	147	+18
Feed grains 1/ 2/	108	84	-22
Rice, milled 1/	22	15	-32
Tobacco, unmfd.	46	44	-4
Veg. oils & seeds	101	100	-1
Soybeans	36	52	+44
Ed. veg. oils 3/	48	37	-23
Fruits & preps.	46	41	-11
Vegs. & preps. 1/	22	21	-5
Animals & prods. 1/	96	94	-2
Fats & oils	29	28	-3
Meats & prods.	19	19	0
Hides & skins	11	12	+9
Dairy products 1/	27	23	-15
Other 1/	14	16	+14
Total	632	686	+9

1/ Includes private relief. 2/ Excludes products. 3/ Cottonseed and soybean.

August exports were somewhat above those of last year. August shipments of $327 million in 1960 were 8 percent larger than the $304 million of a year ago. Commodities that gained included cotton, wheat, soybeans, and vegetable oils. Exports of feed grains, rice, and tobacco were moderately below last August's levels. Shipments of vegetables, tobacco, and animal products continued close to the levels of a year ago.

COTTON Large quantities of cotton are moving into foreign markets. Exports of cotton totaled 0.8 million running bales in July-August 1960 compared with 0.2 million in July-August 1959. Exports of cotton a year ago were extremely low while the 1959-60 payment-in-kind program was getting underway. Prospects are for a continued high level of U. S. cotton exports in the year ending June 30, 1961 although they may be slightly below the 6.6 million bales attained last year, when exports were at the second highest level in 26 years. Foreign production and inventories are somewhat larger this year, but foreign consumption continues at a high level and ample supplies of U. S. cotton are available at competitive prices. Cotton registered under the current season's payment-in-kind program totaled 2.7 million bales as of October 14 compared with 2.6 million last October 16.

GRAINS   Wheat exports were up by one-sixth in July-August. Wheat and flour exports totaled 85 million bushels in July-August 1960 compared with 73 million in July-August 1959. A substantial part of the wheat exports has been moving under Title I of Public Law 480. At present, wheat exports for fiscal year 1961 are estimated at 550 million bushels, which is equal to the previous record established in fiscal year 1957. An increase of 30 to 40 million bushels is expected in exports to Europe this year, following the low-quality wheat harvest there. Exports under Government-financed programs are expected to exceed the 374 million bushels shipped last year.

Europe's large supplies of feed wheat have reduced demand for feed grains. Feed grain exports of 1,934 thousand short tons in July-August 1960 were one-fourth below the level of 2,519 thousand a year ago. Europe, which took over three-fourths of the record U. S. exports in 1959-60, has a plentiful supply of feed wheat following this summer's low-quality harvest and is likely to import about a million tons less U. S. feed grains this year. The outlook for exports to other areas is somewhat brighter because of smaller foreign production and increased foreign consumption.

Rice exports, down in July-August, are likely to be slightly smaller for the year. Exports of rice in July-August 1960 totaled 2.3 million bags compared with last year's first 2-month volume of 3.5 million. Exports for the current fiscal year as a whole are expected to be slightly below the 20.5 million bags shipped last year, the second best on record. A prospective increase in exports to Western Europe is likely to be offset by a further decline in sales to Cuba. Nearly half of total rice exports is expected to move under Title I of Public Law 480.

TOBACCO   Tobacco exports will probably exceed last year's shipments. Exports of 58 million pounds of unmanufactured tobacco in July-August 1960 were down 6 percent from the level of a year ago. However, exports for fiscal year 1961 as a whole are expected to increase by 5 percent, reflecting the larger U. S. crop of above-average quality, stable prices for U. S. leaf, and a rise in foreign cigarette consumption.

VEGETABLE OILS   Continued strong foreign demand for soybeans is expected
AND OILSEEDS   to result in another record export year. Soybean exports of 23 million bushels in July-August 1960 were one-third larger than the 15 million bushel total shipped in the same period a year ago. The continuing strong foreign demand reflects primarily the increased consumption in Japan and the increased crushing in Northern Europe for oil and meal. Shipments for fiscal year 1961 are expected to exceed last year's 133 million bushels.

Exports of vegetable oils are likely to remain high. Exports of expressed vegetable oils (cottonseed and soybean oils) totaled 338 million pounds in

TRADE NEWS ROUNDUP

A new postwar foreign outlet for U. S. tobacco has been opened in Poland as a result of a Title I Public Law 480 authorization for purchases up to $1.5 million. Although Poland has imported no U. S. cigarette leaf since 1939, the Polish Tobacco Monopoly plans to make an American blend cigarette.

―――――――O―――――――

The U. S. agricultural exhibit at the IKOFA Food Fair in Munich, West Germany, September 23-October 2, was awarded a Gold Medal for excellence. The exhibit featured U. S. wheat, rice, poultry, soybeans, fruit, honey, frozen and packaged foods, and ready-prepared food mixes. Some 100 thousand samples of U. S. foods were given out in return for coupons which appeared in local newspapers.

―――――――O―――――――

Title I Public Law 480 agreements announced mid-September to date totaled $51 million. Ceylon--$5.1 million for wheat flour. Ecuador--$1 million for edible vegetable oil. Supplemental agreements: Republic of Korea--$870 thousand for cottonseed oil and/or soybean oil. UAR-Syria--$1.6 million for barley. India--$17.1 million for tobacco, corn, grain sorghums, and soybean oil. Iran--$15.1 million for wheat or wheat flour. Pakistan--$10.3 million for rice.

―――――――O―――――――

The Export-Import Bank has granted a $3.5 million credit for 1960-61 to Austria to finance imports of U. S. cotton. Austrian spinners are expected to buy about 28,000 bales with this loan. Last year $6 million was authorized for the same purpose.

―――――――O―――――――

Russian statistics indicate that the U.S.S.R. imported about 213 million pounds of tobacco in 1959, which would make it second only to the United Kingdom, the world's largest tobacco importer. Imports have been rising fast because consumption is increasing while production is lagging. Russia imports leaf from Bulgaria and Communist China in payment for Russian industrial machinery, petroleum, and manufactured goods.

―――――――O―――――――

U. S. exporters of baby chicks and mixed poultry feeds may benefit from France's recent extension of liberalization measures to Martinique, Guadaloupe, and French Guiana.

―――――――O―――――――

The 38th Annual National Agricultural Outlook Conference will be held November 14-17, 1960, at USDA in Washington, D. C.

―――――――O―――――――

July-August 1960 compared with 376 million for the same period a year ago.
Exports this fiscal year are expected to continue near the high rate of
last year and probably will approximate the record 1,601 million pounds of
1959-60.

FRUITS AND   Fruit exports are likely to be down somewhat this fiscal year.
VEGETABLES   July-August exports of fruits and preparations of $41 million
             declined by 11 percent from 1959 to 1960. Total exports of
oranges and grapefruit in the fiscal year ending June 30, 1961 are expected
to decline from 1960 because of high levels of competitive supplies and
smaller U. S. crops. Canned and dried fruits are likely to increase
slightly because of generally ample supplies available at competitive prices
and trade liberalization measures in Western Europe.

Decline in vegetable exports is seen in small exportable supply of dried
beans. July-August 1960 exports of vegetables and preparations totaled
$21 million, about the same as a year earlier. Major commodities were fresh
and canned vegetables and dried beans and peas. While an increase is expected for fresh and canned vegetables during fiscal year 1961, the gain
will probably be more than offset by a decline for dried beans resulting
from reduced supplies available for export.

ANIMALS AND   A 5-percent value increase is indicated for exports of
ANIMAL PRODUCTS animal products this fiscal year. July-August exports
                 of animals and animal products totaled $94 million in
1960 compared with $96 million in 1959. Indications are that shipments of
dairy products, tallow, poultry meat, beef, pork, variety meats, and hides
and skins will be somewhat larger in fiscal year 1961 than in 1960. Developments contributing to this increase are the large exportable U. S. supplies available at competitive prices, increased foreign consumption, and
trade liberalization measures favoring dollar-area commodities.

I M P O R T   H I G H L I G H T S

Agricultural imports declined slightly during July-August. U. S. imports
of agricultural commodities totaled $650 million during July-August 1960,
3 percent below this period in 1959. The decline can be attributed to a
moderate drop in supplementary commodities which more than offset the rise
in imports of complementary products.

July-August supplementary imports were 8 percent below last year. Imports
of supplementary (somewhat competitive) commodities totaled $330 million
this July-August compared with $360 million during the same period last
year. Major value declines were in cane sugar, 15 percent; dutiable cattle,
70 percent; vegetable oils, 15 percent; and copra, 20 percent.

Imports of complementary commodities gained slightly. Complementary (noncompetitive) imports totaled $320 million during July-August 1960, 4 per-
cent ahead of a year ago. With the exception of crude rubber, increases
were noted for all of the principal commodities.

August agricultural imports were slightly below last year. Imports of supplementary commodities declined 10 percent during the month of August while

complementary products remained relatively unchanged from a year earlier.
August imports totaled $345 million in 1960 compared with $351 million in
1959. Principal supplementary declines were in cane sugar and dutiable
cattle. While imports of coffee were 7 percent below last year, compensat-
ing complementary gains were recorded for silk, carpet wool, bananas, cocoa
beans, tea, spices, and crude rubber.

Agricultural imports are supplied by relatively few countries. Although the
United States imports agricultural commodities from more than 125 countries,
the bulk of the trade is with 19 major countries. In fiscal year 1960 each
of these 19 (see import table below)   supplied over $50 million worth of
U. S. agricultural imports. In total they accounted for more than 70 percent
of such imports. Shipments from the 19 countries ranged from a high of $532
million for Brazil (principally complementary) to a low of $57 million for
Italy (mainly supplementary). During fiscal year 1960, imports increased
from Brazil (mainly coffee), Philippines (sugar), Indonesia (crude rubber),
Australia (beef and veal), Federation of Malaya (crude rubber), India (pepper
and castor oil), and the Belgian Congo (coffee). Major declines were reported for Canada (principally dutiable cattle), Mexico (dutiable cattle,
Colombia (coffee), and Argentina (meat products).

U. S. agricultural imports by country of origin, fiscal years 1959 and 1960

Country	1958-59			1959-60		
	Supple-mentary 1/	Comple-mentary 2/	Total	Supple-mentary 1/	Comple-mentary 2/	Total
	Million dollars					
Brazil	53	465	518	46	486	532
Cuba	423	3	426	422	2	424
Colombia	3/	303	303	3/	266	266
Philippines	214	11	225	235	12	247
Mexico	144	85	229	118	68	186
Canada	238	3	241	181	3	184
Indonesia	1	100	101	1	134	135
New Zealand	99	28	127	95	31	126
Australia	78	1	79	114	3/	114
Federation of Malaya	3/	72	72	3/	114	114
Argentina	97	37	134	52	36	88
Netherlands	22	16	88	66	18	84
India	33	28	61	44	37	81
Thailand	6	59	65	6	61	67
Turkey	57	1	58	62	4	66
Belgian Congo	10	36	46	13	47	60
Guatemala	3/	57	57	3/	59	59
Ecuador	1	52	53	3/	58	58
Italy	52	4	56	52	5	57
Other	461	614	1,075	475	594	1,069
Total	2,029	1,975	4,004	1,982	2,035	4,017

1/ Supplementary imports are somewhat similar to or interchangeable with
domestic products. 2/ Complementary imports are generally not competitive
with domestic products. 3/ Less than $500 thousand.

DOMESTIC EXPORTS: August 1959 and 1960 and July-August 1959 and 1960 1/

Quantity figures in Thousands; Value 2/ figures in 1,000 dollars.

Commodity exported	Unit	August Qty 1959	August Qty 1960	August Value 1959	August Value 1960	July-August Qty 1959	July-August Qty 1960	July-August Value 1959	July-August Value 1960
Cheese*	lb.	831	631	340	295	1,470	1,363	611	647
Evaporated milk	lb.	10,682	6,773	1,640	1,056	27,755	20,811	4,278	3,289
Dried whole milk	lb.	1,393	1,694	852	1,076	3,953	4,095	2,251	2,524
Nonfat dry milk*	lb.	77,347	39,666	6,984	5,439	151,976	94,741	14,601	11,688
Eggs, in the shell	Doz.	1,123	2,034	652	1,031	2,287	4,003	1,417	2,068
Hides and skins 3/	No.	588	986	5,253	6,288	1,199	1,876	10,863	12,376
Beef and veal, total 4/	lb.	2,159	2,596	838	1,014	4,254	4,366	1,665	1,743
Pork, total 4/	lb.	6,825	4,278	2,098	1,116	12,613	7,285	3,704	2,089
Variety meats 5/	lb.	8,317	10,535	1,689	2,360	15,803	18,678	3,277	4,170
Poultry, canned, fresh or frozen 4/	lb.	14,800	16,146	3,993	4,705	25,163	26,829	6,840	7,788
Lard	lb.	39,535	51,186	3,813	5,489	97,900	94,125	9,413	9,855
Tallow, edible and inedible	lb.	108,152	109,764	8,385	7,104	223,167	241,508	17,137	15,741
Cotton, unmfd., excl. linters (running bales)	Bale	98	114	11,019	15,640	227	790	26,451	101,999
Apples, fresh	lb.	3,228	3,035	225	267	7,121	7,876	514	671
Oranges and tangerines, fresh	lb.	45,013	34,126	3,299	2,781	105,989	83,106	7,618	6,283
Prunes, dried	lb.	919	3,576	244	887	2,189	7,769	579	1,927
Raisins and currants	lb.	2,403	7,903	524	808	3,959	10,768	929	1,499
Fruits, canned 6/	lb.	62,385	38,450	8,983	5,071	84,229	54,953	12,254	7,629
Orange juice	Gal.	819	1,095	1,694	1,811	1,641	2,148	3,366	3,742
Barley, grain (48 lb.)	Bu.	14,629	5,769	14,662	5,801	28,573	11,486	28,275	11,774
Corn, grain (56 lb.)*	Bu.	15,854	20,025	21,093	25,676	38,326	35,906	50,211	46,226
Grain sorghums (56 lb.)	Bu.	12,460	10,369	13,263	11,907	20,551	20,056	22,081	22,050
Oats, grain (32 lb.)	Bu.	6,185	3,731	4,140	2,722	15,311	5,722	10,069	4,236
Rice, milled, excludes paddy*	lb.	205,980	75,142	12,737	5,513	348,995	227,671	22,070	15,422
Rye, grain (56 lb.)	Bu.	590	154	703	176	1,023	1,161	1,261	1,157
Wheat, grain (60 lb.)*	Bu.	27,110	34,579	47,944	58,748	61,091	72,150	106,094	122,981
Flour, wholly of U.S. wheat (100 lb.)*	Bag	2,557	3,051	10,876	13,417	5,008	5,435	22,194	23,814
Oil cake and oil-cake meal (2,000 lb.)	Ton	49	59	3,117	3,645	94	97	6,216	6,076
Flaxseed (56 lb.)	Bu.	1,030	231		726	3,379	859	10,490	2,734
Soybeans, except canned (60 lb.)	Bu.	5,222	13,781	12,309	31,541	15,072	22,991	35,502	52,909
Soybean oil, crude, refined, etc.	lb.	102,738	195,669	11,539	21,538	258,124	276,251	29,679	30,098
Cottonseed oil, crude, refined, etc.	lb.	51,027	33,907	7,926	4,600	117,441	61,743	18,513	7,818
Tobacco, unmanufactured	lb.	38,865	37,771	29,270	29,552	61,935	58,331	46,025	44,226
Beans, dried*	lb.	40,801	37,806	3,086	2,778	93,263	61,064	7,163	4,570
Peas, dried except cowpeas and chickpeas	lb.	17,458	15,173	1,072	837	22,617	26,144	1,369	1,432
Potatoes, white	lb.	33,118	11,535	884	309	58,390	59,433	1,685	1,531
Vegetables, canned 6/	lb.	6,375	9,705	996	1,528	14,470	19,770	2,278	3,067
Other agricultural commodities				43,127	42,311			83,289	85,854
TOTAL AGRICULTURAL COMMODITIES				304,479	327,126			632,232	685,703
TOTAL NONAGRICULTURAL COMMODITIES				1,079,642	1,265,378			2,205,839	2,589,200
TOTAL ALL COMMODITIES				1,384,121	1,592,504			2,838,071	3,274,903

1/ Preliminary. 2/ At place of export. 3/ Excludes the weight of "other hides and skins", reported in value only. 4/ Product weight. 5/ Includes beef and pork livers, beef tongues, and other variety meats, fresh or frozen. Product weight. 6/ Includes only classes shown separately in Table 2 of the monthly "Foreign Agricultural Trade".

* Includes "Food exported for relief or charity by individuals and private agencies".

Compiled from official records, Bureau of the Census.

Commodity	Unit								
Olives in brine	Gal.	830	1,388	1,314	1,662	2,010	2,762	3,142	3,?70
Pineapples, canned, prepared or preserved	Lb.	13,438	15,266	1,585	1,765	23,318	28,704	2,798	3,309
Barley, grain (48 lb.)	Bu.	905	714	1,299	865	1,551	1,224	2,151	1,542
Oats, grain (32 lb.)	Bu.	216	102	187	100	313	175	277	182
Wheat, grain (60 lb.)	Bu.	127	271	246	466	478	492	783	816
Feeds and fodders	3/			448	357 3/		3/	1,236	696
Nuts and preparations	3/			6,518	5,795			12,825	11,495
Copra	Lb.	67,012	49,168	6,405	3,688	122,744	132,359	12,535	10,315
Vegetable oils, fats, and waxes, expressed	Lb.	39,167	35,756	7,260	6,062	87,621	77,519	15,906	13,320
Seeds, field and garden	3/			1,374	628 3/		3/	2,425	1,144
Sugar, cane (2,000 lb.)	Ton	437	354	48,277	39,542	962	804	106,329	89,539
Molasses, unfit for human consumption	Gal.	24,838	44,543	2,552	4,016	53,566	94,396	5,432	8,041
Tobacco, unmanufactured	Lb.	13,324	14,919	9,660	11,396	26,805	26,244	19,710	19,451
Tomatoes, natural state	Lb.	804	1,697	58	123	2,078	2,703	147	181
Other supplementary				23,149	24,763			48,021	48,568
Total supplementary				178,647	172,511			359,753	330,809
COMPLEMENTARY									
Silk, raw	Lb.	628	938	2,329	3,945	943	1,497	3,502	6,284
Wool, unmfd, free in bond (actual weight)	Lb.	15,523	16,850	8,289	9,401	33,457	35,099	17,528	19,916
Bananas	Bunch	3,937	4,943	5,368	6,506	8,798	9,088	11,876	12,442
Cocoa or cacao beans	Lb.	28,446	45,090	9,418	11,628	56,655	86,929	18,794	22,309
Coffee (incl. into Puerto Rico)	Lb.	286,296	268,939	99,337	91,815	452,985	487,155	161,047	169,859
Coffee essences, substitutes, etc.	Lb.	320	574	558	1,007	555	711	1,?80	1,246
Tea	Lb.	8,228	9,132	3,743	4,185	17,924	17,716	7,968	8,226
Spices (complementary)	Lb.	7,000	5,345	2,823	3,376	12,437	8,997	4,934	6,033
Abaca or Manila (2,240 lb.)	Ton	2	1	481		6	2	2,706	1,166
Sisal and henequen (2,240 lb.)	Ton	11	8	1,185	1,618	19	15	3,099	3,069
Rubber, crude	Lb.	101,548	88,697	1,771		208,008	152,659	64,019	57,718
Other complementary				32,003	32,745			12,109	11,419
Total complementary				172,666	172,259			308,632	319,687
TOTAL AGRICULTURAL COMMODITIES				351,313	344,770			668,385	650,496
TOTAL NONAGRICULTURAL COMMODITIES				839,359	900,567			1,758,382	1,739,677
TOTAL ALL COMMODITIES				1,190,672	1,245,337			2,426,767	2,390,173

1/ Preliminary. 2/ Product weight. 3/ Reported in value only.

Compiled from official records, Bureau of the Census.

USDA, Agri. Marketing Servi...
1-15-60 Floyd F. Hedlund, Dep. Dir.
FATD Fruit & Vegetable Div.

- 8 -

IMPORTS (FOR CONSUMPTION): July 1959 and 1960 1/

Commodity Imported	Unit	Quantity July 1959 (Thousands)	Quantity July 1960 (Thousands)	Value July 1959 (1,000 dollars)	Value July 1960 (1,000 dollars)
SUPPLEMENTARY					
Cattle, dutiable	No.	46	12	6,345	1,509
Casein or lactarene	lb.	7,976	8,234	1,558	1,581
Cheese	lb.	3,906	3,430	1,984	1,720
Hides and skins	lb.	15,757	14,433	7,100	5,831
Beef and veal, total 2/	lb.	58,432	51,718	20,799	18,720
Pork, total 2/	lb.	15,678	15,584	10,458	10,456
Mutton,goat & lamb,fresh or frozen 2/	lb.	6,774	6,483	1,454	1,489
Sausage casings	lb.	1,502	1,271	1,088	1,025
Wool, unmfd., exc 1 free, etc. (actual weight)	lb.	9,574	7,001	6,003	4,955
Cotton, unmfd., ex. linters (480 lb.)	Bale	5	1	87	82
Jute & jute butts, unmfd. (2,240 lb.)	Ton	5	2	843	289
Olives in brine	Gal.	1,180	1,374	1,926	1,609
Pineapples, canned, prep. or pres.	lb.	9,881	13,438	1,213	1,544
Barley, grain (48 lb.)	Bu.	646	510	852	678
Oats, grain (32 lb.)	Bu.	97	73	90	82
Wheat, grain (60 lb.)	Bu.	351	221	537	350
Feeds and fodders				787	338
Nuts and preparations		3/	3/	6,307	5,700
Copra	lb.	55,732	83,191	6,130	6,628
Seeds, field and garden		48,454	41,763	8,646	7,258
Sugar, cane (2,000 lb.)	Ton	3/	3/	1,051	516
Vegetable oils, fats, and waxes, exp.	lb.	525	450	58,052	49,997
Molasses, unfit for human consumption	Gal.	28,728	49,852	2,880	4,025
Tobacco, unmanufactured	lb.	13,481	11,325	10,050	8,054
Tomatoes, natural state		1,274	1,005	88	59
Other supplementary		3/	3/		
Total supplementary				24,876	23,803
				181,106	158,298
COMPLEMENTARY					
Silk, raw	lb.	315	559	1,173	2,339
Wool, unmfd., free in bond (actual weight)	lb.	17,934	18,249	9,239	10,515
Bananas	Bch.	4,861	4,145	6,508	5,936
Co or co beans	lb.	28,209	41,839	9,376	10,681
Coffee (incl. into Puerto Rico)	lb.	166,689	218,217	61,709	78,044
Coffee essences, substitutes, etc.	lb.	235	137	492	239
Tea	lb.	9,696	8,584	4,225	4,040
Spices (complementary)	lb.	5,437	3,653	2,110	2,657
Abaca or Manila (2,240 lb.)	Ton	4	1	1,521	685
Sisal and henequen (2,240 lb.)	Ton	8	7	1,328	1,451
Rubber, crude	lb.	106,460	63,962	32,016	24,973
Other complementary				6,269	5,868
Total complementary				135,966	147,428
TOTAL AGRICULTURAL COMMODITIES				317,072	305,726
TOTAL NONAGRICULTURAL COMM.				919,023	839,110
TOTAL ALL COMMODITIES				1,236,095	1,144,836

1/ Preliminary. 2/ Product weight. 3/ Reported in value only.

N
LTURAL
Digest
NOVEMBER—
DECEMBER 1960
OF THE UNITED STATES

, Foreign Agricultural Service, United States Department of Agriculture,
).C. Free within U.S. on request. Also available are monthly and
gricultural Trade Statistical Reports, containing detailed statistics
value of exports and imports.

E X P O R T   H I G H L I G H T S

gricultural exports in 1960–61 were 6 percent ahead of
s of U. S. agricultural products in July–September totaled
1 fiscal year 1960–61 compared with $994 million in the
Substantial gains occurred in cotton, wheat and flour,
xports of fruits were slightly above the level in 1959–60.
ere somewhat offset by declines in feed grains, animal
le oils, rice, tobacco, and vegetables.

cultural exports,
ty, July–September

	1959–60	1960–61	Chg.
	Million	dollars	Pct.
	52	128	+146
'	407	425	+4
'	191	246	+29
'/	154	126	-18
	29	21	-28
	116	110	-5
	141	128	-9
	51	72	+41
	66	43	-35
	67	71	+6
	34	31	-9
1/	151	139	-8
	44	40	-9
	29	33	+14
	16	17	+6
/	44	31	-30
	26	23	-12
	994	1,055	+6

ate relief. 2/ Excludes
nseed and soybean.

September agricultural exports
were slightly above those of a
year ago. Exports of $369 mil-
lion in September of 1960–61
were 2 percent above shipments
of $361 million in the same
month a year earlier. There
were increases in wheat including flour and in soybeans. Exports of feed grains, tobacco,
rice, vegetable oils, and animal products were moderately below last September's levels.
Cotton, fruits, and vegetables
remained at about the same levels of a year earlier.

Indications are that fiscal year
1960–61 will be a good one for
agricultural exports. They are
expected to total $4.5 billion,
which is equal to the second
highest figure on record attained
last year. The alltime record
in value was $4.7 billion in

1956-57. Quantity is likely to equal or exceed last year's record volume shipments. More wheat and flour, soybeans, tobacco, and animal products are expected to be exported while a reduction is likely for feed grains, rice, fruits, and vegetables. About as much cotton and vegetable oils are expected to move out this year as last year when the export volume was unusually heavy.

Exports to the 3 largest dollar markets in July-September increased by 16 percent. July-September exports to the 3 principal foreign dollar markets for U. S. agricultural products--the United Kingdom, Canada, and Japan-- increased from $274 million in fiscal year 1959-60 to $318 million in 1960-61. This $44 million gain accounted for nearly three-fourths of the total rise of $61 million for agricultural exports this year. The largest single country gain was the $46 million increase to India, mostly under the Title I of Public Law 480 (foreign currency sales). Other increases occurred in exports to Italy, Belgium, Spain, Pakistan, France, and Denmark. Declines were registered in exports to West Germany, Poland, Venezuela, Cuba, Yugoslavia, Brazil, UAR-Egypt, and Mexico.

COTTON   Exports of cotton this July-September doubled those of the same period in 1959-60. Cotton exports in July-September this year totaled 1 million bales compared with 0.5 million in the like period of 1959-60. Exports in the first quarter last fiscal year were extremely low while the payment-in-kind program was getting underway. Exports in this fiscal year may exceed the 6.6 million bales moved in 1959-60. The continuing high level of foreign consumption, the low level of old-crop stocks in foreign exporting countries, and the ample supplies of U. S. cotton available at competitive prices are helping most to maintain exports this year. Cotton registered under the current season's payment-in-kind program totaled 3.8 million bales as of November 11 compared with 3.6 million November 20 a year ago.

U. S. agricultural exports by country of destination, July-September

Country	1959-60	1960-61	Chg.
	Million dollars		Pct.
United Kingdom	124	130	+5
Canada	89	102	+15
Japan	61	86	+44
India	38	84	+121
Netherlands	78	78	0
West Germany	73	64	-12
Italy	34	38	+12
Belgium	28	31	+11
Spain	24	31	+29
Poland	33	29	-12
Pakistan	9	27	+200
Venezuela	25	24	-4
Cuba	31	19	-39
Yugoslavia	19	16	-16
Brazil	21	16	-24
France	9	15	+67
UAR-Egypt	16	15	-6
Denmark	11	14	+27
Mexico	15	14	-7
Other	256	222	-13
Total	994	1,055	+6

GRAINS   Wheat and flour exports in the July-September quarter this year were nearly one-third ahead of 1959-60. Exports of wheat and flour totaled 142 million bushels in July-September of 1960-61 compared with 108 million in the same period of 1959-60. More than half of the wheat exports this year were under Title I of Public Law 480, principally to India, Pakistan, and Poland. For the year as a whole, exports are expected to equal the previous

TRADE NEWS ROUNDUP

Higher wheat import requirements of Western Europe are expected to contribute significantly to the expected rise of 75 million bushels in the
1960-61 world wheat trade estimated at nearly 1,400 million bushels.
Heavy rains at harvest time lowered the quality of wheat in Northern
Europe, and as a result considerable quantities are suitable only for
feed. Smaller wheat crops in Italy and Spain are also contributing to
larger import needs. The United States is likely to furnish over half
of Europe's increased import requirements this year. Some parts of Asia
had larger crops, but India and Pakistan continue to have their usual
large import requirements.

———————————0———————————

Recent livestock sales in Italy have demonstrated the ready market there
for animals bred from U. S. bulls. Twenty head of under-1-year-old
U. S.-sired bulls were sold this September at the Cremona (Italy) International Livestock Show at prices averaging $800 a head.

———————————0———————————

The recent purchase of 7,000 tons of U. S. wheat by a new flour mill in
Angola was a direct result of an on-the-spot market development survey
and promises to give the United States a dominant place in the country's
wheat market. Before the mill was built, the United States was a major
exporter of wheat flour to Angola.

———————————0———————————

The highly successful campaign to sell more U. S. tallow to Japan is in
its third year. Tallow and grease exports have risen from 205 million
pounds in 1955 to an estimated 340 million in 1960, a gain of 66 percent.
Indications are that Japan could replace Italy as the No. 1 U. S. foreign
market for tallow and greases although the Netherlands also is a strong
contender for first place. U. S. tallow and greases are currently among
the least expensive fats entering world trade.

———————————0———————————

The Tariff Commission has scheduled public hearings February 7 and 8 in
Washington, D. C. to determine if cantaloupes and watermelons, respectively, are being imported in such increased amounts because of concessions granted under the General Agreement on Tariffs and Trade as to
cause or threaten serious injury to the U. S. industry. "Escape clause"
action is provided by law in the event such concessions are injurious.

———————————0———————————

Title I Public Law 480 agreements announced since mid-October: Viet Nam--
$7.5 million for wheat flour and cotton. France--$2.5 million for tobacco.
Indonesia--$16 million for rice, cotton, and tobacco. Greece--$13.7 million for wheat, feed grains, and vegetable oils. Chile--$28.9 million for
wheat, feed grains, cotton, edible vegetable oil, and tobacco. Supplemental agreements were announced with Uruguay--$3.2 million for corn and Iran--
$1.2 million for cottonseed oil or soybean oil.

record of 549 million in 1956-57 and to be well above the 512 million bushels shipped last year. A substantial increase is expected in dollar exports to Western Europe which had a poor quality harvest in the past season. Italy and Spain, wheat exporters in recent years, have to import this season, and the United States will supply a sizable part of their requirements. Shipments under Government-financed programs are also likely to increase slightly. In the Near East, continuing drought during the past season has increased the import needs of that area. India and Pakistan are expected to require larger quantities this year. In addition to the increased demand in foreign importing countries, lower wheat availabilities in a number of minor exporting countries also will contribute to larger U. S. shipments.

Rice exports lagged in the first quarter of fiscal year 1960-61. Milled rice exports this July-September totaled 3.1 million bags compared with 4.4 million in July-September of 1959-60. Over two-fifths of the decline represented smaller shipments to Cuba. Total exports of rice in fiscal year 1960-61 as a whole are expected to be slightly below the 20.5 million bags exported last year, the second best on record. A sharp decline is expected in shipments to Cuba while Western Europe and Asia will take considerably more.

First quarter feed grain exports to Western Europe fell substantially this year. Exports of feed grains in July-September this year totaled 2.9 million short tons compared with 3.5 million tons in the same quarter of 1959-60. Western Europe took 0.7 million short tons less this year than last. The downturn in U. S. exports is expected to continue for several months. Larger production of corn and other feed grains in many importing countries and the use of low-quality wheat for feed in Western Europe have lessened foreign requirements this year.

TOBACCO   July-September tobacco exports this year were below those in 1959-60. Unmanufactured tobacco exports this July-September of 141 million pounds were 10 percent below the 156 million pounds in the same months of 1959-60, when exports were unusually heavy in anticipation of a dock strike. Total exports this fiscal year are expected to be about 5 percent above the 457 million pounds moved last year. The expected increase reflects the larger U. S. crop of above-average export quality, stable prices for U. S. leaf, and a rise in foreign cigarette consumption.

VEGETABLE OILS   More soybeans are continuing to move into foreign markets.
AND OILSEEDS   Exports of soybeans in July-September of 1960-61 totaled 31 million bushels compared with 22 million in July-September of 1959-60. Demand for U. S. soybeans in Japan and Western Europe continues high. Japan's consumption of soybeans has increased appreciably, and Western Europe has been crushing more beans for meal and oil. Total exports in fiscal year 1960-61 are expected to exceed last year's record of 133 million bushels.

Vegetable oil exports this year were below those in 1959-60. Exports of cottonseed and soybean oils in July-September this year totaled 383 million pounds compared with 528 million in the same quarter of 1959-60. However, increased foreign consumption without an accompanying rise in foreign production is expected to result in record exports of U. S. vegetable oils in fiscal year 1960-61.

FRUITS AND   Fruit exports gained while vegetable exports declined this year.
VEGETABLES   July-September 1960-61 exports of fruits and preparations
               totaled $71 million, 6 percent more than a year ago, and those
of vegetables and preparations totaled $31 million, 9 percent less than in
July-September 1959-60. The increase in fruit exports reflected the ample
U. S. supplies of dried fruits available for export and less foreign competition this year. Smaller exports of dry beans accounted for most of the
decline in the vegetable group.

ANIMALS AND   Exports of animal products were down slightly. July-
ANIMAL PRODUCTS September 1960-61 exports of animals and animal products,
                 including USDA donations, totaled $139 million, 8 percent
less than the $151 million in the first quarter of 1959-60. Exports of
tallow, lard, and dairy products fell somewhat while those of meats and hides
and skins gained.

                 IMPORT   HIGHLIGHTS

Agricultural imports during the first quarter of fiscal year 1960-61 were
well below the level attained last year. July-September imports of agricultural commodities totaled $961 million this year, 12 percent below those in
July-September 1959-60. Declines occurred in both supplementary and complementary commodities.

July-September supplementary agricultural imports totaled $482 million this
year, $69 million below a year ago. All of the major commodities either
declined or showed relatively little change during the first quarter this
year. Cane sugar and beef and veal imports accounted for the major part of
the decline in supplementary takings.

Complementary agricultural imports totaled $478 million during July-September
1960-61, 11 percent below this period last year. Imports of complementary
commodities, which were slightly ahead during the first 2 months of the
fiscal year, dropped off sharply during September, accounting for the lower
July-September total. Decreased coffee and crude rubber imports contributed
most to the lowering of the complementary total.

July-September coffee imports this year were smaller compared with the same
period last year because the then-threatening dock strike encouraged a
buildup in domestic stocks. This year, with domestic stocks at normal levels
and abundant supplies available abroad, roasters have been hesitant to increase their importations. Sugar imports, which have recently undergone a
change in their source of supply, are lagging behind last year although they
are expected to pick up and may exceed the level recorded in 1959-60.

Imports of agricultural commodities declined sharply during September. Agricultural imports totaled $310 million this September, 26 percent below a year
ago. Both supplementary and complementary commodities showed lower totals,
21 percent and 30 percent, respectively, below the previous year. Major
declines were in coffee, cane sugar, crude rubber, and beef and veal, with
most other commodities remaining unchanged or showing a lower total.

NOTE: In the table on page 1 of the October DIGEST, 1958-59 and 1959-60
       should read 1959-60 and 1960-61, respectively.

DOMESTIC EXPORTS: September 1959 and 1960 and July-September 1959 and 1960 1/

Commodity exported	Unit	September				July-September			
		Quantity		Value 2/		Quantity		Value 2/	
		1959	1960	1959	1960	1959	1960	1959	1960
		Thousands	Thousands	1,000 dollars	1,000 dollars	Thousands	Thousands	1,000 dollars	1,000 dollars
Cheese*	Lb.	621	636	287	322	2,090	2,000	898	969
Evaporated m k* l	Lb.	9,275	6,237	1,473	1,002	37,029	27,048	5,751	4,290
Dried who e m k	Lb.	2,798	1,734	1,571	1,009	6,752	5,830	3,822	3,533
Nonfat dry m k*	Lb.	68,153	27,824	7,515	3,757	220,130	122,565	22,016	15,445
Eggs, in the shell	Doz.	1,188	1,829	657	992	3,475	5,832	2,074	3,060
Hides and skins 3/	No.	530	863	4,834	5,042	1,730	2,739	15,698	7,4 B
Beef and veal, total 4/	Lb.	2,729	2,756	989	1,068	6,983	7,121	2,654	2,81
Pork, total 4/	Lb.	6,546	7,103	1,816	1,908	19,159	14,388	5,520	3,997
Variety meats 5/	Lb.	8,711	11,373	1,863	2,357	24,514	30,051	5,140	6,527
Poultry, canned, fresh or frozen 4/	Lb.	15,188	22,279	4,378	6,548	40,351	49,108	11,219	14,336
Lard	Lb.	57,279	42,319	5,219	4,513	155,179	136,444	14,632	4,368
Tallow, edib h and inedible	Lb.	121,755	92,260	8,973	6,016	344,922	333,769	26,111	21,757
Cotton, unmfd., excl. linters (running bales)	Bale	230	193	25,601	25,855	457	983	52,053	127,854
Apples, fresh	Lb.	11,599	11,014	963	979	18,720	8,889	1,477	1,650
Oranges and tangerines, fresh	Lb.	34,636	22,029	2,559	1,844	140,625	05,34	10,177	8,127
Prunes, dried	Lb.	2,697	6,994	649	1,782	4,886	14,763	1,229	3,708
Raisins and currants	Lb.	5,070	27,670	1,019	3,393	9,029	38,439	1,948	4,892
Fruits, canned 6/	Lb.	45,412	79,217	5,986	10,540	129,641	134,170	18,240	18,169
Orange juice	Gal.	839	1,011	1,784	1,586	2980	3,159	5,150	5,329
Barley, gra h (48 lb.)	Bu.	11,254	9,394	11,06	9,767	39,827	20,879	39,881	21,541
Corn, grain (56 lb.)*	Bu.	15,762	13,624	20,720	17,432	54,088	49,530	70,931	63,659
Gra h sorghums (56 lb.)	Bu.	8,846	9,920	9,854	10,666	29,397	29,976	31,935	32,716
Oats, grain (32 lb.)	Bu.	2,261	5,297	1,485	3,857	17,572	1,020	11,555	8,093
Rice, milled, excludes paddy*	Lb.	90,701	80,319	6,471	5,172	439,696	307,990	28,541	20,594
Rye, gra b (56 lb.)	Bu.	467	491	544	515	1,490	1,652	1,805	1,672
Wheat, gra h (60 lb.)*	Bu.	27,737	48,550	48,188	83,997	88,328	120,701	154,282	206,978
Flour, wholly of U. S. wheat (100 lb.)*	Bu.	3,374	3,513	14,218	14,921	892	8,948	36,413	38,735
Oil cake and oil-cake meal (2,000 lb.)	Ton	68	68	4,330	4, 67	162	165	10,546	0,248
Flaxseed (56 lb.)	Bu.	1,346	123	4,361	387	4,724	982	14,871	3,121
Soybeans, except canned (60 lb.)	Bu.	6,714	8,164	15,495	8,617	21,786	31,155	50,997	71,526
Soybean oil, crude, refined, etc.	Lb.	135,406	30,325	14,92	3,615	393,53	306,576	44,671	33,712
Cottonseed oil, crude, refined, etc.	Lb.	16,654	14,795	2,620	1,767	34,095	76,538	21,132	9,585
Tobacco, unmanufactured	Lb.	93,654	82,922	70,288	66,234	155,589	141,253	116,312	110,460
Beans, dried*	Lb.	33,952	33,446	2,769	2,540	127,215	94,421	9,932	7,110
Peas, dried (except cowpeas and chickpeas)	Lb.	29,028	20,286	2, 09	1,470	51,645	46,430	3,378	2,903
Potatoes, white	Lb.	23,157	7,369	611	247	8,547	66,802	2,296	1,778
Vegetables, canned 6/	Lb.	8,205	8,671	1,230	1,205	22,675	28,440	3,508	4,272
Other agricultural commodities				51,377	42,354			134,661	128,209
TOTAL AGRICULTURAL COMMODITIES				361,324	369,443			993,556	1,055,147
TOTAL NONAGRICULTURAL COMMODITIES				1,102,879	1,224,977			3,308,719	3,814,177
TOTAL ALL COMMODITIES				1,464,203	1,594,420			4,302,275	4,869,324

1/ Preliminary. 2/ At place of export. 3/ Excludes the weight of "other hides and skins", reported in value only. 4/ Product weight. 5/ Includes beef and pork livers, beef tongues, and other variety meats, fresh or frozen. Product weight. 6/ Includes only classes shown separately in Table 2 of the monthly "Foreign Agricultural Trade".
* Includes "Food exported for relief or charity by individuals and private agencies".

Compiled from official records, Bureau of the Census.

Commodity imported	Unit	Quantity 1959 (Thousands)	Quantity 1960 (Thousands)	Value 1959 (1,000 dollars)	Value 1960 (1,000 dollars)	Quantity 1959 (Thousands)	Quantity 1960 (Thousands)	Value 1959 (1,000 dollars)	Value 1960 (1,000 dollars)
SUPPLEMENTARY									
Cattle, dutiable	No.	22	9	2,623	1,247	89	31	11,983	4,088
Casein or lactarene	Lb.	8,517	5,131	1,630	976	22,214	19,796	4,264	3,795
Cheese	Lb.	6,724	5,045	3,533	2,611	14,244	12,857	7,345	6,628
Hides and skins	Lb.	18,448	8,815	8,994	4,030	44,579	32,656	21,393	14,517
Beef and veal, total 2/	Lb.	88,618	48,636	31,011	16,975	217,267	171,088	77,219	61,313
Pork, total 2/	Lb.	12,101	12,568	8,003	8,760	39,664	41,379	25,711	27,826
Mutton, goat and amb, fresh or frozen 2/	Lb.	4,193	2,209	963	552	13,861	14,545	3,089	3,454
Sausage casings	Lb.	1,166	1,496	945	1,111	3,923	4,135	2,881	3,286
Woo l unmfd., e cxl free, etc. (actual weight)	Lb.	9,842	6,269	7,862	4,599	29,255	58,000	20,302	17,415
Cotton, unmfd., e cxl linters (480 lb.)	Bale	24	22	3,134	2,799	123	113	19,413	19,846
Jute and jute butts, unmfd. (2,240 lb.)	Ton	4	4/	391	68	12	3	1,526	498
Olives in brine	Gal.	1,017	1,408	1,484	1,672	3,027	4,169	4,626	4,942
Pineapples, canned, prepared or preserved	Lb.	9,317	7,298	1,144	835	32,635	36,002	3,942	4,143
Barley, gra h (48 lb.)	Bu.	1,292	204	1,721	279	2,843	1,429	3,872	1,821
Oats, gra h (32 lb.)	Bu.	144	127	135	117	457	303	412	299
Wheat, gra h (60 lb.)	Bu.	538	391	916	693	1,016	883	1,699	1,509
Feeds and fodders		3/	3/	451	264	3/	3/	1,686	959
Nuts and preparations				7,419	6,637			20,244	18,131
Copra	Lb.	61,588	75,442	5,394	5,457	184,332	207,801	17,930	15,772
Vegetable oils, fats, and wa es, expressed	Lb.	47,331	51,599	8,071	7,522	134,952	129,118	23,977	20,841
Seeds, f e H and garden		3/	3/	1,558	649	3/	3/	3,984	1,793
Sugar, cane (2,000 lb.)	Ton	461	367	50,945	41,321	1,423	1,172	157,274	130,860
Molasses, unf l for human consumption	Gal.	24,821	36,992	2,731	3,106	78,387	131,387	8,164	11,147
Tobacco, unmanufactured	Lb.	11,656	13,335	8,572	9,907	38,462	39,578	28,282	29,358
Tomatoes, natural state	Lb.	310	1,442	18	129	2,388	4,144	165	310
Other supplementary				31,689	29,170			79,207	77,744
Total supplementary				191,337	151,486			551,090	482,235
COMPLEMENTARY									
Silk, raw	Lb.	1,022	616	3,891	2,669	1,966	2,113	7,393	8,953
ool, unmfd., free in bond (actual weight)	Lb.	23,530	17,654	12,828	9,431	56,987	52,753	30,356	29,347
Bananas	Bunch	4,085	4,395	5,929	5,922	12,883	13,482	17,804	18,364
Cocoa or cacao beans	Lb.	41,651	39,453	14,362	9,795	98,306	126,382	33,156	32,104
Coffee (nc l into Puerto Rico)	Lb.	402,714	259,700	136,922	87,510	855,699	746,855	297,969	257,370
Coffee essences, substitutes, etc.	Lb.	381	297	644	542	937	1,008	1,695	1,788
Tea	Lb.	7,264	9,132	3,433	4,745	25,188	26,848	11,401	12,971
Spices (complementary)	Lb.	7,911	5,268	3,006	2,629	20,348	14,265	7,940	8,662
Abaca or Manila (2,240 lb.)	Ton	3	1	1,078	445	9	3	3,784	1,610
S sal and henequen (2,240 lb.)	Ton	12	7	1,827	1,462	31	23	4,926	4,530
Rubber, crude	Lb.	106,977	71,351	35,014	25,581	314,985	224,010	99,034	83,299
Other complementary				8,947	7,983			21,055	19,403
Total complementary				227,881	158,714			536,513	478,401
TOTAL AGRICULTURAL COMMODITIES				419,218	310,200			1,087,603	960,696
TOTAL NONAGRICULTURAL COMMODITIES				929,457	848,924			2,687,839	2,588,601
TOTAL ALL COMMODITIES				1,348,675	1,159,124			3,775,442	3,549,227

1/ Preliminary. 2/ Product weight. 3/ Reported in value only. 4/ Less than 500.

Compiled from official records, Bureau of the Census.

Lightning Source UK Ltd.
Milton Keynes UK
UKHW051902231118
332685UK00028B/248/P

9 780260 633194